The Cost of Loving

The Cost of Loving

Women and the New Fear of Intimacy

§

Megan Marshall

G. P. Putnam's Sons
New York

Library of Congress Cataloging in Publication Data

Marshall, Megan.
The cost of loving.

1. Single women—United States—Case studies.
2. Single women—United States—Attitudes. 3. Women in
the professions—United States—Interviews. 4. Intimacy
(Psychology) I. Title.
HQ800.4.U6M37   1984   305.4′890652   83-17795
ISBN 0-399-12859-X

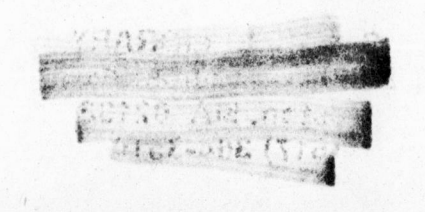

For John

Acknowledgments

It took the help of many people to complete this book. First were the friends and relatives who kindly put me up during my research travels: Sandra Caskie, Bob and Betsy Crosby, Charles Dawe, Anne Fadiman, Gillian Johnson, Patti Manby, Elva Marshall, Emily Sedgwick, Fan Sedgwick, and Lou Ann Walker. Cynthia Castle was the careful listener who transcribed many of the interviews I brought back with me.

It would be safe to say that this book would never have been written without the encouragement of my agent, John Brockman, who was the first to believe in the project. As I worked through the manuscript, the advice of Joanne Wyckoff, Anne Peretz and George Vaillant inevitably came when it was most needed. My editor, Diane Reverand, has been the perfect combination of sympathetic listener and clearheaded analyst. And no one could have asked for a better reader and editor than my husband, writer John Sedgwick.

My deepest thanks must go, however, to the forty women who spoke to me about their lives with such candor and trust, and without whom my work would have been impossible.

Contents

On the day when it will be possible for woman to love not in her weakness but in her strength, not to escape herself but to find herself, not to abase herself but to assert herself—on that day love will become for her, as for man, a source of life and not of mortal danger.

Simone de Beauvoir
The Second Sex, 1952

Prologue: Living by the Code

I began asking the questions that led to writing this book during a conversation with a friend who, after seven years of medical training, would soon become a pediatrician. I had always admired Nina for her skill in the sciences, for her choice of such a useful and demanding profession, and especially for her calm efficiency in treating patients. Without ever becoming unapproachable, she had managed to fulfill many of the ideals my friends and I had held up to each other since we met in college in the early 1970s. Although her life at times seemed to have narrowed to the circuit between the hospital where she worked and her tiny studio apartment in downtown Boston, Nina seemed to us to be succeeding in the best of all possible ways: on her own.

But when we met for dinner this evening in the early spring of 1980, she was upset. I had just asked about her plans for starting up a medical practice when her residency ended—and Nina had confessed she had none. "Setting up a practice is an entirely different step from applying to medical schools or residency programs," she told me, her calm deserting her. "It's a decision about how I'll be spending *the rest of my life*."

Nina had always imagined she would set up a practice with another doctor—her husband—in a small town where the two could bring up their children. "With my training I could go anyplace in the country," she said. "But there's no reason to *go* anyplace. I'm afraid I'll end up in some town where I won't find a man, and I'll never have a family." The decision that once promised liberation from the solitary years of medical apprenticeship was now forcing Nina to recognize just how limited her choices had become. "I don't want to be alone anymore," she almost whispered, "but I don't know how to get involved. It's the first time I've been able to admit this—and already it seems too late."

I was stunned. Not just because I hadn't expected to hear worries like these from Nina, but because I realized there was no answer to them in the code our generation lived by—a code made up of feminism, professionalism, and philosophies of self-fulfillment in roughly equal parts. We were silent as we both suddenly understood that her problems would not be solved by the standard line we used in times of conflict: "Do what's best for *you*, and everything else will fall into place." My friend and most of the women we knew had made countless youthful decisions by putting ourselves first. And where had it gotten Nina? Now that she felt ready to make a choice that would include others— a man, a family, a community—she had none of these to choose from. Nina was bright and attractive, and had never lacked male companionship when she wanted it. Yet, as she at last was forced to admit, something about the way she conducted her love affairs had kept her from forming a lasting attachment. The fate we all dreaded most, that our personal lives would disrupt our careers, was now coming to pass for Nina in a way she had never imagined possible: not because she had a lover who was too demanding, but because she had no one who demanded anything of her at all.

Several days later another friend, a psychologist who had lived with a man for over five years, told me she could not possibly consider marrying her boyfriend until she concluded a major research project, which she expected to last several years. The emotions a wedding would stir up might interfere with her work, Carolyn explained. If I hadn't just been talking to Nina, I'd have agreed with Carolyn right off. Instead I heard in her determination a second law of the code: after "Do what's best for *you*" comes "Careers can't wait, but men can." Suddenly I found myself asking Carolyn what made her so certain her boyfriend would be that patient. And was she really gaining anything by putting off an event that even she recognized would be emotionally significant? Even assuming the relationship could be put on hold, Carolyn's research could also suffer if she continued to dawdle over making such an important personal commitment.

I began to wonder whether our generation's wisdom, intended to make us more powerful, both professionally and personally, than the women who raised us, wasn't actually holding us back. I found out for myself how much of our code was based on fear rather than on high ideals when, later that spring, my boyfriend of three years asked me to marry him. In the code that meant he was planning to turn me into a housewife, a wageless slave, a suburbanite, a 1950s Mom—all the dirty words I could think of. But could this man who had already treated me fairly for over three years, and had never once suggested I quit my job, be guilty of such an intention? When *he* asked me to marry him, my boyfriend assured me, all he meant was, "I love you—I want to live with you for a long time." Yet our code had so perverted the language of love that a straightforward proposal of marriage seemed like a jail sentence.

I tried hard to think of marriage his way. But our code had no bylaws for decisions involving love; marriage was all but taboo. None of my friends could name a woman whose life hadn't gone downhill after her wedding. Certainly our mothers, mainly housewives or career women who willingly played second fiddle to our fathers, offered no shining examples. And nearly every book or movie we cared about described in precise detail the inevitable dehumanization of the average American husband and wife. But could I say no to marriage just because it had harmed a good many women in the past? Wouldn't that be nearly as wrong as repeating the bad patterns themselves? When at last I said yes it was as much because it seemed cowardly to reject an offer that frightened me so much as because I was in love.

In the summer of 1980, I joined the sudden rush of women who, in their late twenties, had decided to marry, reversing for the first time in a decade the downward trend in American marital statistics. But for most of us marriage wasn't easy. Our weddings were attended by disapproving single women friends who accused us of desertion. We went off on honeymoons suffering from acute anxiety over lost independence, scarcely comforted by the decision to keep our maiden names when we returned to work. For months afterward, I remained outwardly apologetic with many of my single friends about the relationship that inwardly I knew was supporting me in more important ways than my job ever could. Still, I continued to have no ready answer to their suspicious questions about marriage, no words to convince them that I wasn't falling into a state of cowardly and petty domestic dependence.

When I started the interviews that form the basis of this book it was with the simple aim of finding the words to describe this period of confusion and contradiction that most of the women I knew seemed to be entering as the ideals of feminism, professionalism and self-fulfillment increasingly failed us. By listening to and recording the words of other women, I hoped to document what I suspected were the growing pains of an entire generation, of which the breakdown of the code was only the first symptom.

To do this I left Boston and traveled to Atlanta, Houston, Los Angeles, San Francisco, Chicago, Washington and New York where I conducted lengthy interviews with forty single working women. Aged twenty-six to thirty-seven, they are women of the baby boom. Most were raised by affectionate housewife mothers who nevertheless did not prepare their daughters for the world they would grow into. Unlike many of their mothers, nearly all of the forty went to college and stayed there until they had earned one, and in some cases, several degrees. Now these women are architects, lawyers, doctors, artists, journalists, newscasters, bankers—or receptionists and waitresses still trying to figure out what to do with their educations, but never questioning their right to do *something*.

I spoke to each woman for several hours, covering in as much detail as possible her personal and professional history. I wanted to find out the way each woman viewed the shape of her life, where it had come from and where it would lead her. Because of the intimate nature of their confidences, I have changed the names and other distinguishing details of the ten women whose lives I have written about at length. And, although it is a practice generally out of favor with journalists, I have in several cases created composite characters when the events of a particular woman's life would have certainly betrayed her identity. The events themselves, as well as all issues and attitudes that came up in these interviews, are described exactly as they were reported to me.

I chose to write a book about single professional women because they are the special product of our generation. There are now more single women between the ages of twenty-five and thirty-five than ever before in America. Many of these are the women who have pioneered in professions previously barred to women. Although they are not the majority, single professional women became our generation's role models and standard-bearers. They are the New Women. As such their lives demonstrate the unique blessings and burdens of our generation in their most dramatic forms: the new wealth of financial and professional achievements, as well as the new impoverishment of personal commitments. They have taken the greatest advantage of the new freedom of choice—and they are now living with the consequences.

Away from home and on the road, I was delighted to feel a part of the single culture, once again the equal of women who, by taking adventurous jobs and living on their own, had become the heroines of our generation. But when I began hearing from so many of them the same belated doubts and self-defeating code words that Nina, Carolyn and I had tangled with during the past year, I knew I wanted to do more than document the breakdown of our code. I became more than ever convinced that our generation needed to re-examine its ideals, to find new words for new hopes and ambitions before, as Nina had feared, it was too late.

Many of the women I spoke with were facing crucial decisions about love and work made impossible by the code we lived by. Or, like Nina, they were feeling a sudden and overwhelming emptiness because they had so little left to decide about. The burnt-out, have-it-all superwoman is as much a stranger to these women as the run-down house-wife: many felt, looking back, they had never had much at all.

The case studies in this book are colored by extreme regional differences as well as by differences of tempera-ment and of ambition. Yet together they add up to evidence of a problem deeper than the failure of our code and closer to a full-scale crisis in female identity, played out in opposi-tions of our own devising: work and love, independence and dependence, self and others, assertiveness and compro-mise. Our generation has reached a turning point that few of us had expected and none was prepared for. This crisis, which is forcing young women everywhere to reassess their lives, is what *The Cost of Loving* is all about.

PART I
The New Fear of Intimacy

"And what do *you* do?"—came the question for what seemed like the fifteenth time that night. It was the summer of 1981 and I was in Arcadia, California, attending the tenth reunion of my high-school class. It was the first time many of us had seen each other since crossing the border from adolescence into adulthood. Crowded around the buffet table or dancing to golden oldies played by a small-time rock band, the hundred or so men and women in the darkened function room were scarcely recognizable as the boys and girls with whom I'd grown up in the 1960s in a large public school system several towns away. Tonight the men were taller, their hair shorter and their beards longer than when I'd seen them last. Women were wearing slacks, once banned by our school dress code, and many looked trim and muscular in a way we would certainly have found unattractive in that prejogging era. But it was that question—"What do *you* do?"—asked over and over again by the women as we reacquainted ourselves, that registered the greatest change of all.

Our campus was as hip as a high school could be in the late 1960s. There were student walkouts, drugs, free sex, racial violence. But women's liberation was still unknown to us. No one questioned the fact that girls were cheerleaders and boys were football players. Girls liked poetry and boys liked math. Even among the campus flower children, girls embroidered blue jeans for the boys who wore them. Girls were the helpers, the onlookers, the appreciators. Boys were the doers.

After graduation we had scattered to all parts of the country, some of us marrying, many of us entering college. Yet we women had all come back to Southern California ten years later asking the same question of each other, a question that would never have occurred to us when we were in school together: "What do *you* do?"

The answers were sometimes thrilling. Among us there were a photojournalist, an actress, a graphic designer, a geologist, a reading specialist, a therapist for the emotionally disturbed—all genuine triumphs for women whose mothers, when they were our age, had confined their activities to running Girl Scouts or the PTA. But there was an anxious tone to much of our shoptalk, one that could not be explained away as the natural competition at a class reunion. It was as if, no matter what we were doing, it wasn't enough.

I heard it first in the words of several women who had given up "doing" to raise children. They answered the question of the evening with apologies: "I'm planning on going back for my master's this year," or, "I'll be looking for a job as soon as Jimmy is out of diapers." Many of the class mothers went home, I found out later, without once reaching for the snapshots of their children they'd brought along in their pocketbooks.

And they weren't the only women concealing evidence of their personal lives. In an earlier decade, showing off husbands would have been standard fare at a class reunion. Yet few of my married classmates had brought their husbands to tonight's party. In all their talk of "doing," most omitted any reference to weddings or marriage.

It was the single women—and there were a good many of them—who seemed to have nothing to be ashamed of. Yet there was no less anxiety in their voices, no less evasiveness about personal affairs. As they spoke, sometimes condescendingly to those who had withdrawn from the workaday world into marriage and motherhood, there was a weariness to their descriptions of tight deadlines, business trips, and battles for promotions, that betrayed a diminishing faith in the working world as well as a hopelessness about alternatives. I knew from the few friends I'd stayed in touch with over the years that the facade of professional competence only thinly concealed the private wounds: disappointed loves, compulsive promiscuity, lesbian experimentation, abortions, divorce, and just plain loneliness. Though they were doing the most of anyone there, doing itself was beginning to seem like not enough. "I never thought I'd be saying this," said one single friend as we drove home from the party, "but I envy those women with families. They think I've got it all figured out just because I have a good job—but they don't know how much I'd give to find a man who I could live with for longer than a weekend."

Still, I knew my friend was only half serious. She would return to her job and continue trying to live up to the standards of professional achievement and personal deprivation that seemed to be driving our entire generation. To all of us, "doing" had achieved some kind of undeniable significance, loving and caring were signs of weakness and defeat. Where once, as women, we would have shared anecdotes about husbands and children, we had played, instead, the standoffish one-upmanship of a men's club. Those of us who hadn't managed to avoid marriage and motherhood actually found ourselves apologizing for what were once the central facts of a woman's life. Married or single, mothers or not, all of us had cultivated a by now instinctive self-censorship that kept us from talking about our personal lives—a silence that covered, as in my friend's case, a deep ambivalence about the value of love in a working woman's life.

As I traveled around the country later that year, interviewing the forty single women whose case studies provide the data for this book, I recognized again and again the same anxiety, the almost crippling distrust of the personal combined with a growing disappointment with the professional, that I had seen in the faces of my classmates. I found myself asking, What kind of women have we become? What was this ideal of worldly achievement and personal sacrifice we were all trying to live up to? Where did it come from—and why weren't we listening to the anxiety in our voices and in our hearts?

The Myth of Independence

Ours was a generation of women determined to learn from our parents' mistakes. Believing we could solve the problems that had confined women to their kitchens for decades past, we had developed our own world-weary philosophy by the time we had turned twenty. If woman's total devotion to husband and children had kept her from developing her own potential, ran the popular ideology, our solution would be to cut off family ties and grow free. We watched our mothers made helpless by their dependence on our fathers, and we vowed never to marry. We saw our mothers grow depressed and centerless as housewives, and we determined to prove ourselves in careers. We suspected our mothers of having dull sex lives, and we planned to keep our own lives free of stultifying commitments. We even told ourselves that if we ever changed our minds and decided to marry, we'd be better off for our years of independence: the stronger we were as individuals, the better chance we'd have of making a good marriage.

In this atmosphere of reform and revolution, the Myth of Independence was born. The liberation movements of the 1960s and 1970s fed our belief in the curative powers of independence. We invented names to dignify every one of our newly discovered indulgences, made up philosophies to rationalize our fears. If we worked long hours, craving professional success, it was in the name of Equal Rights. If we took a different man to bed every night, it was in the name of Sexual Liberation. If we grew suspicious of those men and stopped going to bed with them, it was in the name of

Feminism. If we became territorial, protective of our apartments, our evenings, our privacy, it was in the name of Self-Discovery.

Month after month, our new way of life was celebrated in magazines designed especially to meet the needs of a new market: ourselves. In their pages the Myth of Independence was solidified into a code by which we could live our daily lives. *Working Woman* and *Savvy* told us where to shop for the right navy blue suit, when to trade in a pocketbook for a briefcase, and how to tell a lover you won't leave your job to follow him to another city. *Cosmopolitan* taught us which men to pick up in singles bars, and how to have an orgasm on a one-night stand. With its title, *Ms.* reminded us in every issue that we were not to define ourselves by relationships with men, just as *Self* informed us we had an alternative.

Soon there were millions of single and newly divorced women descending on urban centers across the nation determined to live the Myth of Independence. The less our mothers had worked, studies would later show, the more hours we would put in at our highly prized entry-level jobs. Still, we had time to find each other in chic restaurants on our lunch breaks where we discussed our bosses and competitors over quiche and salad. We formed women's groups and met weekly in our apartments or in church basements to support each other in our careers and to defend ourselves against the demands of men. Working against centuries of conditioning, we learned to tell ourselves that what *we* wanted was best—and we tried to find out what that was. As we agonized over options, gloried in successes and suffered setbacks, we always told ourselves that men could wait. Families could wait. For a long time we didn't even feel lonely. We had our new women friends, and it seemed that the husbands and children who had been promised to us by parents and grandparents, teachers and school advisers since we were little girls had just been put on hold, a set of actors waiting in the wings till we called for them.

Yet everywhere I was finding more and more evidence that Independence wasn't working. The anxiety I'd noticed

among the women of my high-school class was taking over.
In 1982 I traveled across country interviewing the front-
runners of our generation—the single working women who
had lived the Myth of Independence to the fullest. I visited
them in high-rise condominiums and renovated town
houses in Boston, Washington, Chicago, and New York; in
singles complexes in Atlanta and Houston; in funky Vic-
torian frame houses in San Francisco and in compact Spanish-style bungalows in Los Angeles. There, amid the
exposed brick and African ferns, I found the women who,
according to the Myth of Independence, should have been
the proudest and most satisfied of us all: the women who,
all by themselves, at thirty or thirty-five, were making partner in law firms, writing feature stories for the nation's top
newspapers, running entire businesses from their tastefully
furnished living rooms. But every one of these women was
struggling to quiet a growing fear that all this was not
enough, that the Myth of Independence had led her astray.
As one woman finally admitted, "I was always secretly
longing for some of that dependence the women's movement was saying we shouldn't need. Now I keep asking
myself, what was wrong with wanting someone else in your
life you can count on?"

"You'd think my life was ideal," confessed a high-
powered lawyer. "I have a great job, a wonderful apartment, enough money to be self-indulgent. But you run and
run and run and then you wake up one day and you're
twenty-nine and a half and you say, 'What do I have to
show for it?' There is not a damn thing I don't have—
except the one thing I want more than anything else. A
man. As much satisfaction as I get out of my job, it just
doesn't keep me warm at night."

The Myth of Independence was leaving women dangerously unprepared for their changing emotional needs
as they reached their thirties. Another woman, who
had turned down several proposals of marriage in her mid-
twenties believing she should concentrate her energies on
advancement within a corporation, explained, "We all believed that our personal lives and our careers would track

along together. Marriage would come when our careers had peaked. Now I'm secure enough in my career to get married, but there are no men in my life, and I realize that's largely because I've put all my efforts into my work. They don't teach you to fall in love at Stanford Business School!"

The Myth of Independence, it turned out, wasn't even helping some women find themselves. "I never know whether I'm acting in my own best interest or for some abstract notion of what *women* should do," admitted a thirty-two-year-old lawyer who left her marriage to devote herself to her career, only to find herself confronting an emptiness of a different sort. "I sometimes find myself fantasizing about living the rest of my days on a big farm, making jam and tomato preserves—but then some voice inside says you can't give up, you can't let *women* down. But then I wonder whether I'm not really letting my*self* down." Even women who had become experts at putting themselves first were no better off, for in every city I visited women were growing impatient with the self-centered ethic of the Myth of Independence. "Every day I wake up alone and ask myself, What kind of acid did I take to choose a life like this?" said an anchorwoman for a major urban network. "I'm tired of thinking about me, me, me!"

But there was no place to turn. If a woman was lonely, according to the Myth, it was because she was weak, probably not ready for marriage anyway. Wanting a man was a sign that something was wrong: a modern woman should enjoy solitude. The Myth of Independence drew her inexorably on, away from love, away from the intimate trusting relationship that might have assuaged her loneliness. No one asked, anymore, whether falling in love might help a woman find herself. Every book or magazine she read, every movie she saw, underlined the same theme: that the search for self was the primary goal of a woman's life and that she must do it alone. In *Kramer vs. Kramer* a woman walks out on her husband and child and gets away with it by uttering the magic words, "I have to find out who I am." On television, Mary and Rhoda and Alice, Laverne and Shirley became our heroines: single women who proved to us week after week that men might be worth toying with, but life is more interesting without them. Marriage, these shows implied, was dull, confining, never romantic, and never self-affirming. Love was always opposed to self-knowledge, marriage and motherhood the enemy of self-revelation.

In the Myth of Independence, there was no sympathy for "I'm tired of thinking about me, me, me!" It was a complaint that could never be uttered. We all knew that Prince Charming was a fairy tale—but did we ever stop to think that Independence might also be a hoax?

The Control Generation

In 1971, the year my high-school class went on to college, a nationwide survey found that only one in five freshmen women planned to become a housewife after graduation, and scarcely half of those four remaining planned to marry. That same year, the valedictorian of Mills College announced in her graduation address that, "The best thing I can do for mankind is never to have children." What did we want instead of marriage and motherhood?

We had gone off to college in record numbers not, as so many of our mothers had, to find husbands, but to find ourselves. "My experience of going away to college," one woman told me, "was to discover that I was a person for the first time. After growing up in a traditional family where women didn't count for much, I felt as if this huge oppressive shroud had been lifted off me and I could live like I had a life of my own. I certainly wasn't in any rush to get attached to somebody, and I certainly wasn't even going to consider getting married."

Once found, we would not let ourselves go. After college we wanted to work, to support ourselves and never to be in debt to a man or obligated to children. Above all we wanted to be in control of our fates in a way our coupon-cutting, recipe-collecting, husband-dependent mothers never had been. One popular writer, Rosemary Ruether, expressed the desperate need for a release from motherhood we all felt. "Each generation of women has been sacrificed to its own children," she wrote in *New Woman New Earth*. "History has been the holocaust of women." We were determined to be the generation that survived.

At college we took our place in a nationwide student community that chose to live life on its own terms, terms we invented as we went along. We wanted "control" of our bodies, and we demanded free dispensation of contraceptives on our campuses so we would not be inhibited by fears of pregnancy. We wanted to be strong and fearless, so we signed up for "survival" courses in the wilderness, "self-defense" courses in the cities, and "assertiveness training" courses in the office. Then we proved ourselves by taking jobs that once only men were considered physically or intellectually fit to perform. We put on hard hats for construction jobs, business suits for the law and corporate finance, lab coats for medicine and the sciences.

If biology was destiny, we'd work on changing biology. We made ourselves infertile with birth control pills and sealed off our wombs with diaphragms. We lobbied for abortion rights, and nearly half of us would have an abortion sometime during our childbearing years. The bestselling *Our Bodies, Ourselves*, the primer of our new sexual awareness, pictured women straddling their lovers during intercourse. The daughters of the Smith College graduates who had inspired Betty Friedan to write *The Feminine Mystique* marketed the famous centennial T-shirt emblazoned with: SMITH COLLEGE: A CENTURY OF WOMEN ON TOP. In another popular book of the time, *The Dialectic of Sex*, Shulamith Firestone envisioned a utopia in which women would be entirely freed of childbearing functions by the invention of artificial wombs. This was the world we thought we wanted, a world with women in control, free from physiological limitations, free from the demands of men and children. "We're the control generation," said one woman as she related her fantasy of freeze-drying her children for raising in her forties or fifties "when I'm ready for them." It was a time, as in the beginning of all revolutions, when anything seemed possible.

For a while, the self-controlled life-style triumphed. Throughout the 1970s, marriage and birth rates dropped steadily. The number of women living alone between the ages of twenty-five and thirty-five tripled until by 1980 the total number of single women in our age group surpassed five million. At mid-decade, surveys of the national well-being showed that single women were the most content of all adult groups. They were more intelligent and capable than single men, happier than housewives, more satisfied with their lives, even than married working women. Pollsters suspected it was because single women never suffered from the disease that magazines and newspapers dubbed "role strain"—the stress of answering the often contrary demands of playing mother, wife and worker. Single women had only themselves to answer to.

But the gains of the Control Generation turned out to be only partial. We felt strong as we went about our work, proud to be accepted as the equals of men in a man's world. But around the edges of our lives, anxiety was creeping in. As we reached our thirties, whether from an instinctual desire to be mated or from what feminists would argue was the socialization of a sexist culture, we began to feel something was missing. Although magazine articles and books and movies and television shows continued to celebrate her, the single self-directed woman wasn't so happy anymore. In 1981, when *Savvy* magazine surveyed its readers, a group of women that likely derives greater than normal satisfaction from work, its single readers reported they were the least content with their lives of all groups. Work was no longer enough. Independence had outlived its usefulness.

The same year, *Cosmopolitan* ran a full-page ad in *The New York Times* that revealed the bind single women were finding themselves in as they passed from the 1970s into the 1980s. "Loving is *easy*," said a buxom brunette in a low-cut peasant blouse. "I love my folks, friends, little brother, cats, split-leaf dracaena and you *could* include my job, New York City and Westhampton when it sizzles. Finding somebody to be in love *with* is the challenge." The single woman was suffering from the opposite of role strain: a shortage of demands. In this vacuum, for which she was prepared neither by the example of her housewife mother nor by the code words of the Myth of Independence, her emotions were going haywire. I heard again and again from women in every part of the country these same words of love for work and apartment and city and friends—anything but the object of a mature passion—amounting to a syndrome in which feelings were transferred to things a woman could control or to people who would never make demands that might cause her to lose control. Yet the more she "loved" her job, her apartment, her plants, her friends, the harder it became to love a man. She might be disappointed in her life devoted to work, ready to stop thinking about me, me, me!—but everything the Control Generation believed in worked against romance.

According to the Myth of Independence she was doing the right thing. "My favorite magazine says surround yourself with loving people," the ad continued, "love them back and forget the 'search' . . . that's how romantic love finds you." We had still not gotten beyond the find-yourself-by-yourself, men-can-wait philosophies that had driven us since our college days. Yet in the pages of the same women's magazines, "the great man shortage" was being heralded as the greatest crisis since the Pill was suspected of being carcinogenic. Because of the year-by-year increase in the birthrate during the baby boom, combined with the continuing trend for men to marry younger women, the male-female ratio in our generation was so severely imbalanced that population experts estimated that only four of ten women still single at age thirty were likely to find mates. For a woman with an advanced degree or a high salary, the odds were the worst. She would find that most of the men in her income bracket were already married. Unless she fell for a younger, less experienced man—a pattern increasingly common, though still not popular with highly motivated women—the higher she rose in her job, the lonelier she would be. With the statistics slanted against her, did it make sense for a woman to play a waiting game?

But the Control Generation was suffering from worse problems than demographics. Even when we met men, we were having trouble loving them. From my interview subjects I began to hear of a problem that women of the sexual revolution had never expected to confront: frigidity. Despite often prolific sexual activity, many women could not have orgasms with their lovers. It was embarrassing. Women of our mothers' generation had been frigid because they believed in sex for reproduction not recreation, and because they had not taken control of their bodies and learned to understand female sexual response—or so we told ourselves. But if we could control our bodies, sometimes we went too far in controlling our emotions. The women who spoke to me about sexual problems were unable to have orgasms because they could not submit to their feelings; they felt incapable of the trust that made passionate lovemaking safe. They could not lose control long enough to permit out-of-control feelings.

Conflict had settled deep into our souls, making us unable to love even when we wanted to.

The Crisis of Female Identity

Why should love come so hard to the Control Generation? The answer lies deeper than the false promise of the Myth of Independence, deeper, even, than the fear of losing control. The answer rests in our fundamental ambivalence about what it means to be a woman, an ambivalence that pits love against achievement, caring against doing, emotion against competence.

Recent changes in the economy, education and health care have freed women from lives devoted to childbearing and homemaking. Yet the women of the Control Generation continued to view the question of how they should spend their adult lives as a matter of mutually exclusive choices. We believed we were starting life with a clean slate: we had erased the past and the future was ours. Yet on that slate the answers we wrote were often simple reversals of the answers our own mothers gave.

"When I was little," a successful bank manager told me, "I always assumed I'd grow up to be like my mother—a plump, happy woman with my husband and children at the center of my life. But around age fifteen I began to see the price she was paying for living her life that way. Her children had started to resent her for living through them, she had no skills of her own to fall back on, and she was growing very bitter about it all, which was starting to turn my father off. She had had everything a woman was supposed to want—everything, I think, that *she* had wanted—but she was losing it all because she had never taken the time to consider herself apart from the family. So around that time another vision came into my mind: this was a woman in tweeds and carrying a briefcase, who was slim and tremendously sexy but attached to no one. Suddenly that was the woman I wanted to be, and there was no place in my mind for that first woman, except sometimes in my nightmares."

Nearly all the women I interviewed, even those who had working mothers, reported a similar change in models from childhood to adolescence. The vision of a mother inseparable from her family was replaced by a working woman attached to no one; a dream of giving was replaced by a dream of doing; a life defined by connections to others was replaced by a life of solitary self-exploration. Inevitably, I learned, the second vision eclipsed the first, the self-motivated woman in tweeds—or in a painter's smock or doctor's coat—promising release from a life of selflessness in the home. A good many of the women I interviewed had lived up to that second vision, learning to wear the tweeds and carry the briefcases of success as if they'd been born to them.

But they hadn't been, and that was the whole problem. Whether because the earlier dream could not be forgotten, or because it represented something basic to female nature, by the time I interviewed these women in their late twenties and thirties, parts of the mother image were beginning to haunt the woman in tweeds. "Some days I look in my closet full of carefully tailored suits, simple blouses and blue jeans for the weekend," admitted a thirty-two-year-old lawyer, "and it makes me very sad. I don't think I'd ever feel comfortable in frilly clothes again—but it's as if there's some part of me that I've had to hide even from myself." Further, a thirty-one-year-old stockbrocker had begun to identify that woman with the briefcase as the source of her problems in love. "One day I realized that when I was all suited up for work I was the very antithesis of the kind of woman I wanted to be," she confided. "My friends and I had gotten into the habit of blaming men for not being able to fall in love with professional women, for feeling threatened by us. But then I began to think about the image I was presenting—and I realized I *was* threatening. It would take X-ray vision for a man to see through this woman in a gray flannel suit steamrolling down Wall Street with her briefcase and discover the part of me that wanted to fall in love."

Like many others, she was beginning to sense that the image of the woman in tweeds left out and even conflicted with something important. Everywhere I went women were describing a feeling that the self-reliance they had worked so hard to achieve was in direct competition with the love and generosity they identified exclusively with the mother image they had rejected since adolescence. But the conflict wouldn't go away by exchanging tweeds for chiffon. The war between the two images of womanhood— the competent worker versus the selfless mother, the single woman versus the loving wife—had spread into other aspects of behavior and would not easily be put to rest. A television newscaster admitted that she realized her compulsive promiscuity was not, as she once believed, helping her find true love. Yet she was unable to stop herself. "The sort of woman who settles down with one man and raises a family still frightens me as much as it attracts me," she said. "My job, my life-style, my love life are all lived in the same way—packing as much as possible into every moment. I'm realizing the fast-food life isn't making me happy in the long run, but if I give up part of it, I'm afraid I'll have to give up all of it." She still found herself, as soon as she got close to one man, calling up another.

An ardent feminist confided that she felt hopeless about

finding a man she could love, explaining, "Almost nothing escapes my detector now—I can't turn it off." Yet she longed for "some middle ground where I could meet a man and not always be doubting him, or turning his words against him. But I'm so afraid if I start ignoring the little things—his football games, his sloppy housecleaning—I'll get sucked into a relationship like my mother's where all the big things went wrong." A third woman, who had several times shared apartments with her lovers only to feel lost in the closeness and break off the relationships, said, "For me, it's beyond conflict—it's all or nothing. I hate the way I lose my independence when I'm with a man. I start giving up my reading time, my women friends, my overtime at the office. Intimacy swallows me up. But I don't want to spend my whole life alone either."

The same women who at first told me that men, with their endless demands for time and understanding, housework and affection, were the greatest threat to a woman's independence, feared even more their own inner impulse to compromise—an impulse that many equated with femininity. Because compromise and the eventual loss of selfhood was so much a part of their mothers' models of love and marriage, they had rejected love itself—and with it the whole package of old-style femininity. One woman after another told me stories of the ways their mothers had given to their families till they had nothing left. Love seemed to their daughters only the first step to a life of gradual self-annihilation in marriage and motherhood. They did not know how to give without giving up.

As many psychologists have said, the one thing in a person's life that never changes is the gender he or she was born with. Part of growing up for a girl is coming to terms with womanhood. Yet for the women of the Control Generation, the old ways of womanhood, based on loving and giving, seemed dangerous. The new ways, centered on achievement and solitary self-discovery, seemed suddenly limited. No one could reconcile the woman in tweeds with the woman in the apron and come up with a unified vision of an adult woman. I asked each of the women I inter-

viewed to define "woman" for me, and nearly all insisted
first that "women are strong, decisive, powerful and capable." Yet as soon as they had uttered those words they
corrected themselves with "*but* women are also compassionate, caring, giving, more thoughtful than men." Although
sometimes the order was reversed—"women are caring, *but*
strong"—the same characteristics were invariably grouped
in opposition. It seemed that the woman who was both
strong *and* caring, decisive *and* compassionate, loving *and*
doing, did not, and could not, exist. Just when we thought
we were free to find ourselves, we were in the midst of a
crisis about womanhood itself.

What did the oppositions mean—the apron versus the
business suit, caring versus doing, the mother versus the
worker? Was one image right and the other wrong? If we
were hearing the gentle voice of the mother in us, did it
mean that the way we had lived our adult lives so far was a
mistake?

Women of the Control Generation came of age in a time
when woman's fundamental character and capabilities were
more hotly debated than perhaps ever before in history.
Beginning in the universities and quickly spreading to the
national media, it was a debate conducted in terms that
made the crisis of female identity inevitable. One of the first
to raise her voice was the psychologist Matina Horner, later
named president of Radcliffe College. In 1972, after a decade of research on motivation problems in college-educated women, Horner published her landmark study,
"Toward an Understanding of Achievement-Related Conflict in Women." Coining the phrase "fear of success,"
Horner questioned for the first time in a systematic way the
value of many attributes once presumed to be innately feminine. Curious to know why it was that so many qualified
women failed to pursue careers, Horner asked female students at a large Midwestern university to complete a story
which began with the statement, "At the end of first term
finals, Anne finds herself at the top of her medical school
class." Most college women, Horner found, responded

negatively to the statement, writing that Anne's report card must have been a mistake, or, worse, that Anne would conceal her grades, deliberately fail in her second semester courses, or even drop out of medical school because academic success might cost her popularity with men. Fear of success was so widespread, Horner wrote, that she could only conclude that in most young women success conflicted with femininity.

Horner's study was in many ways simply a highly sophisticated proof of a lesson in survival that women had passed on from one generation to the next for centuries: let the man win. The difference, this time, was that Horner's study, phrased as it was in terms of women's failure to compete, inspired a generation of women to prove that being female did not have to mean losing out. Horner's findings were written up in *Time, Newsweek, The New York Times Magazine, Ms.*, and countless other magazines and newspapers across the country. "Fear of success" became catchwords with the Control Generation, a phrase we muttered to ourselves whenever we sensed ourselves working or studying less, growing reluctant to ask for promotions, or apologizing for our achievements. We were determined to let nothing—and often that meant no man—stand in our way. Love took on a political connotation: it was what too many women had traded away success for. "Romantic love," wrote the popular writer Caroline Bird in *Born Female*, "[is] a put-up job utilized to trap women into giving up their identities." Femininity, associated as it now was with failure, became a dirty word. We descarded the trappings—the frilly clothes and alluring makeup—in favor of blue jeans and business suits. But most of all we despised the traits of femininity, the passivity and emotionalism that cost us points in the marketplace. We dreamed of becoming the tough professional who had none of the crippling personal commitments to husband and children that most women made in their early twenties. Then we would not be forced to choose between work and love, success and femininity. We would conquer fear of success by avoiding the situations that might produce it—not by dropping out of competition as women had in the past, but by shunning relationships that might compromise our new loyalty to ourselves. "Fear of success" was all we needed to convince ourselves it was right to reject the "plump, happy mother" image wholesale.

Research psychologists began to look for further proof that society had turned femininity into a losing proposition. In the early 1970s, Inge Broverman designed a series of tests to find out how the psychological establishment viewed women. Broverman asked a group of male and female clinical psychologists to check off on a list of personality traits those that applied to healthy men, to healthy women, and to healthy adults. Both male and female psychologists checked off radically different traits describing women and men. Women were "nurturing, generous, dependent, fearful, overemotional, passive," whereas men were "aggressive, assertive, bold, independent." Most alarming was Broverman's finding that none of the characteristics used to describe women had made it onto the list describing a healthy adult. Apparently America's psychologists, the people responsible for the nation's emotional well-being, believed that women never displayed the attributes of healthy adults. Worse, if a woman did appear "aggressive, assertive, bold, and independent," she would be judged unhealthy.

Broverman's work and other similar studies fueled our determination to prove that women could be anything but "nurturing, generous . . . overemotional, passive"—the traits that, presumably, had kept women subservient for generations. Why shouldn't women learn to be bold and aggressive? we asked, never caring that we had just tossed aside all the qualities that once defined womanhood. But these were the days of "unisex" hairstyles and clothing, when to speak of differences between the sexes meant being branded a sexist. Even the trait once considered most fundamental to women, the maternal instinct, came under attack as women struggled to shrug off the notion that femininity was little better than a congenital defect. Several noted psychologists wrote papers, popularized in Ellen

Peck's *The Baby Trap*, arguing that the maternal instinct was a hoax perpetrated by a sexist society to keep women out of positions of power. The accusations about femininity were easier to live with if we believed the traits were imposed on us rather than innate.

We began reading a series of handbooks that taught us how to acquire the traits necessary for assimilation into the male power structure. In *How to Make It in a Man's World*, Letty Cottin Pogrebin echoed Matina Horner: "The fear of sacrificing femininity at the altar of success has kept thousands of girls 'in their place.'" Betty Harragan's *Games Mother Never Taught You* capitalized on the popular belief that if a woman mastered the rules of the playing field and the marketplace she could—and should—take her place alongside men in the legions of the successful. Laws were passed—Title IX in sports and affirmative action guidelines for the workplace—to make it all possible. We tried hard to measure up to the new standards, never stopping to think that we had simply exchanged woman's attributes in favor of man's, never asking if we might be giving up something of value.

Was it possible to wipe out in one generation what centuries of women had thought and felt? Was it even desirable? As the women of the Control Generation went off to prove themselves in a man's way in the man's world, a second wave of psychologists entered the debate in the late 1970s. Setting out to discover more about woman's basic nature—what woman *is* rather than what society had made her—these researchers came up, ironically, with many of the feminine attributes the Control Generation had rejected. Horner's fear-of-success study was among the first to be challenged. Taking a stand against the notion that women should change in order to fit into the business world, Georgia Sassen charged in an article called "Success-Anxiety in Women," published in the *Harvard Educational Review*, that it was not success that Horner's college students feared, but rather the competitive situation in which only one person, the woman, was the winner. The problem with Horner's study, according to Sassen, was its definition of success. In the home, the realm in which women traditionally excelled, winning and losing were irrelevant. One mother could succeed without other mothers failing. Some of the best values of the home, Sassen argued, are those of acceptance and empathy that women offer to their families as refuge from the hard-knocks world of the workplace. The reason women avoided competitive situations was not fear of winning, but simple distaste for the whole process.

Other researchers began questioning Broverman's interpretation of sex-role stereotypes. If psychologists judged healthy adult women "nurturing, generous . . . overemotional, passive," Carol Gilligan argued in a 1979 essay, perhaps they *were:* it was society's problem that those qualities were viewed as handicaps. Speaking up for the first time in almost a decade in favor of recognizing sex differences, Gilligan at Harvard and Nancy Chodorow at the University of California proposed a dual model of human development—one male and one female—based on what they perceived as man's fundamental desire for independence and woman's for what they called "inter-dependence." The modern woman's problems derived from trying to fit into a man's world when she wasn't like men after all: equality had been confused with uniformity.

The male model, Gilligan and Chodorow argued, had already been described in classical psychoanalytic theory. Freud had traced the origins of man's drive for independence to the need to break away from his mother in early childhood in order to identify with his father as he grew to adulthood. Erik Erikson based his entire theory of man's life cycle on this premise, arguing that the desire for independence carried through to young manhood in a stage called the "identity crisis." Most young men, Erikson believed, would instinctively fear intimacy and crave isolation during this crisis as they struggled to develop a sense of self separate from relationships, usually by finding a suitable career. Forming close ties with a woman before securing his adult identity would only prevent the young man from realizing his potential both as a worker and a lover: early intimacy would resemble his infantile dependence on his mother at the same time as it burdened him with domestic responsibilities. This distinctive pattern of development, marked by repeated separations from women and chronic fear of closeness, according to Gilligan and Chodorow, explained the masculine traits of assertiveness and independence that turned up in Broverman's study.

Women, on the other hand, need close relationships to find themselves. Nancy Chodorow traced this difference in development to early childhood and the mother-daughter bond. While their brothers had to reject ties with their mother in order to grow up, girls were never confronted with such a conflict, Chodorow argued in *The Reproduction of Mothering*. Women had cultivated the qualities of nurturing and generosity that appeared in Broverman's findings because they grew up imitating their mothers, women whose chief function was caring for a family. Chodorow didn't see this mimicking in the unfortunate political terms that the Control Generation had, but rather as an inevitable and worthy destiny as long as women are mothers and men are fathers. The qualities of nurturance are so deeply embedded in the female psyche, she believed, that women need never undergo an identity crisis such as men regularly experience. While for a man the conflict between self and others is an inescapable part of growing up, for a woman it is her role within relationships that tells her who she is. A woman, driven by her need to find herself in connections with others, in Chodorow's view, need never fear intimacy.

But where did all this leave the Control Generation, the women who had done all they could to avoid turning out like Mom? It was easy to see our double image of womanhood—the single woman in tweeds versus the plump, happy mother—as embodiments of the two styles of development that had divided the experts for more than a decade and that Gilligan and Chodorow had ultimately labeled male and female. But what and whom were we to believe? Was the Myth of Independence a denial of femininity—or simply, as for men, a stage on the road to mature intimacy?

Were we the worst sexists of all, as some psychologists have charged, because we aspired to a male life-style? Are we doomed to shuttle back and forth between male and female models of development, never feeling complete?

I believe that, while the dual model of male and female development may be adequate for explaining the lives of men and women for much of this century, it is not enough to help the women of the Control Generation resolve their conflicts about work and love, intimacy and independence. Women born during the 1950s *are* different from other generations, different from the female type that Gilligan and Chodorow so narrowly defined. To understand the new woman we must look at history and the radical changes that have taken place in women's lives in less than one hundred years.

It would surprise the single professional woman to hear that her mother, the stay-at-home housewife whose life seems so restricted by contemporary standards, was part of a women's movement of her own. It might surprise her even more to realize, as she blames her mother for providing such a poor role model, that perhaps only three generations of women before her have had much choice about how to spend their adult lives. Historians now identify an abrupt turning point in the lives of women: the year 1890 when federal census statistics record for the first time that a majority of American women lived through and even beyond their childbearing years. For centuries, women had been imprisoned as much by disease, malnutrition and poor medical care, as by male sexism. Because the infant mortality rate was also high, childbearing had become woman's most crucial task in order to ensure the survival of the next generation. Yet many women gave their lives in the effort; few survived it.

The historian Kathryn Kish Sklar has documented the tentative movements toward liberation of the first generation of women with the freedom of good health and long lives. Among these women were America's first feminists, Elizabeth Cady Stanton and Susan B. Anthony, who urged

women to take their place alongside men in the world outside their homes. But according to Sklar, who studied
diaries, letters and population records from the late nineteenth century, the majority of these first women with
choice aimed simply to improve the work they were already
doing: mothering. Women in the mid-nineteenth century
began practicing birth control, mainly through celibacy,
not to free themselves from the mother role, but to devote
their best energies, now that improved health care ensured
their infants' survival, to raising three or four children
rather than nine or ten. Would it be fair to call these women
unimaginative or antifeminist because they glorified motherhood? Sklar doesn't think so. These women took pride in
revolutionizing the work that was their special province: the
nurturance and education of new generations.

Our mothers and grandmothers were their offspring,
women who, through the hard years of the Depression and
two world wars, sought to perfect and preserve the art of
homemaking. The mothers we condemn as selfless victims
of a "feminine mystique" were carrying out a movement as
idealistic as any the Control Generation dreamed up—it
just happened to be a dying movement. Betty Friedan
wrote in 1963 that "a woman today who has no goal, no
purpose, no ambition patterning her days into the future,
making her stretch and grow beyond that small score of
years in which her body can fill its biological function, is
committing a kind of suicide." And she was right. Yet it
was the first time that Friedan could have been right for the
mass of women. The medical advances that freed women
from disease and early death in childbirth, that assured
them of their children's survival, had finally made woman's
age-old career as baby maker obsolete.

The Control Generation inherited the nurturing skills
that Gilligan and Chodorow declared basic female traits at a
time when they were no longer so well-suited to women's
daily lives. We could now spend our time more produc-
tively outside the home, working in offices that required an
entirely different set of skills. Matina Horner's fear-of-success study—which would have achieved the same results at

any time in the last hundred years—found such an enthusi-
astic following in the 1970s because for once the let-the-
man-win reasoning behind fear of success hurt women
more than it helped. In an overpopulated world, childbearing ceased to be a crucial task. Finding a man and keeping
him became a matter of choice rather than necessity.

These conditions produced the Control Generation, a
generation with more choices than women had ever
dreamed of, more choices than many of us, looking back,
really wanted. Said one thirty-five-year-old management
consultant, "I envy the women who will come after us.
They won't wake up every morning questioning their role
in society, their role as women. They won't be asking
themselves every day when they look in the mirror, 'Who
am I?' We're the guinea pigs, and we're suffering for it."
Whether or not one generation can provide the answers,
Dr. Janet Surrey, a Boston psychotherapist whose practice
is made up largely of single women asking just those questions, believes that young women today are suffering
through an agonizing personal crisis for the first time in the
history of womankind. "There are so many women in their
twenties and thirties coming to me with conflicts about love
and work, closeness and independence, that women have
never experienced before," Surrey explains, "that I'm beginning to think women are going through a whole new
developmental stage." Certainly, contrary to the Gilligan-
Chodorow model, more women than ever before are finding themselves in their work rather than in relationships.
And more women are suffering the consequences.

The New Fear of Intimacy

For as long as there have been families, women have been
experts in the realm of the emotions. Women understood
their children's needs before their infants could speak;
women soothed men's nerves; women comforted, cajoled,
sympathized, loved. Yet a new generation of women have
deliberately made themselves strangers to emotion. As I
traveled around the country talking to the women of the

Control Generation, I heard numerous tales of women who were unable to break off difficult relationships with men because, as one woman said, "I can't take the time off from work to figure it out." When I asked women what made them happy, often they listed activities they could do alone: working or reading at home, swimming or jogging. When I pressed them to talk about what went on in their relationships with men, many seemed bewildered as they tried to discuss what once had been the staple of women's conversations. Most expressed a good deal of emotion when they described their work, but later, as I listened at home to over one hundred hours of tape from these interviews, in which forty women spoke candidly of all aspects of their lives, I was startled to realize that the word "love" almost never surfaced in connection with a man.

The Control Generation grew up believing that woman's greater capacity for understanding and compassion had made her a second-class citizen, a doormat, a shoulder to cry on, rather than an active member of society. The vulnerability of passion had cost women dearly in the past. Now the women I interviewed were reacting to increased intimacy, usually initiated by the men in their lives, with desperate measures. "The first time a man asked me to marry him," one thirty-year-old woman boasted, "I immediately applied to journalism school and left town." Whether it was by moving away, dating unsuitable men, maintaining impossibly high standards for lovers, or a dozen other diversions, women were becoming experts at rejection and avoidance. The closest many of us came to "inter-dependence" was living with a man. Even then, according to Tufts University psychologist Dr. Jean Wellington, most cohabiting couples break up because the woman moves out, a fact she finds ironic since most women's parents fear their daughters will be the deserted ones.

For a time, avoidance had its benefits. Women discovered new strengths in themselves that had nothing to do with the emotions. "The professions were so exciting to all the women I know," a literary agent told me, "that we were like sponges, just soaking up the experience, reveling in new feelings of power and competence. And we got very selfish about it—we didn't want anything to interfere. I know plenty of cases where men were just pleading with women friends to get married and start a family. Their lovers weren't even asking them to quit work, but they would have none of it." But other women acknowledged the fear that underlay this single-minded drive for achievement. A woman's efforts to keep men out of her life often seemed to increase in direct proportion to her feelings of insecurity. "I was afraid that if I fell in love," one woman said, "I'd immediately be zapped into the suburbs and be losing points off my IQ daily. It was hard enough trying to prove myself at work—I didn't feel ready to stand up for myself in a relationship." And another woman confessed, "I was so insecure about my performance at work that I was terrified of letting anyone get close enough to find out." Fear of success was behind us; fear of intimacy was the new epidemic.

As Gilligan and Chodorow point out, fear of intimacy was once an exclusively male problem. Now women have borrowed it from men, along with business suits and briefcases. And while the new female fears resemble those of men struggling to establish an adult identity, in women fear of intimacy is often both more severe and more prolonged. Because women are new to the working world, and because that world has often been hostile to them, their period of adjustment is usually longer and more stressful. Few of the women I interviewed stayed in one job or even one profession for more than several years, as they searched, with no one to guide them, for their proper place in the job market. Then, in women's lives, love and work have historically been opposed. It was inevitable that women would feel they had to choose between them, even if no one was asking them to. For men, work has always been a stepping-stone to marriage. Women had to invent the Myth of Independence, an ideology which allowed them to start ignoring the demands of others and begin paying attention to themselves, just to get themselves out of the kitchen. While men instinctively knew fear of intimacy would pass, many women of the Control Generation adopted it as a way of life. And when men eventually decided to marry, they never had to ask themselves whether they were setting a bad example for mankind, or whether they were compromising the struggle for man's independence. Women tormented themselves endlessly with such questions. Just when women were facing some of the most crucial decisions of their personal lives, the movement that had brought them so far left them alone with their fears.

For the Control Generation, the major decision of our lives is turning out to be not which career to pursue, but whether to give up some of our newfound self-love to love others. We are suffering from a deep suspicion of our innermost natures that is destroying our relationships as it alienates us from our emotions. Women everywhere are beginning to ask what has gone wrong with their relationships with men, but few have asked whether the Myth of Independence, with its promotion of the solitary woman and the threatening and threatened man, has anything to do with it. This is where we must start if we expect to solve the "I'm tired of thinking about me, me, me!" syndrome. The movements of the past decade have set us free, yet we must learn to make better use of that freedom if we hope to assuage the hopelessness that a twenty-nine-year-old Manhattan lawyer, Ellen Barnes, admitted when she told me, "As much satisfaction as I get from my job—it just doesn't keep me warm at night."

PART II
Brave New Women

I have met brave women who are exploring the outer edge of human possibility, with no history to guide them.

—*Gloria Steinem, 1972*

In the winter of 1973, I left college and migrated, along with hundreds of other dropouts and recent college graduates, to Harvard Square. We filled spare rooms in communal houses or stayed with friends in their dorms until we found jobs that allowed us to move out on our own into the "real world." A nineteen-year-old from California, I learned the ropes from a new set of friends and roommates who even then I thought of as the Brave New Women. They were the confident, intense women in Levi's and work shirts taking entrance exams for law or medical schools. They were the women standing on street corners, defiantly braless in their loose-fitting T-shirts, hawking feminist tracts to support free clinics and women's centers they'd founded in the city's low-rent neighborhoods. They were the long-haired beauties in full skirts and peasant blouses who moved in with men and moved out again, scarcely shedding a tear, leaving a trail of heartbreak behind them. I'd have found Brave New Women in any city from New York to San Francisco. But despite their obvious kinship and their willingness to share ideas and offer advice, Brave New Women were on their own. In those days I only admired their isolation; self-sufficiency was the goal we all aspired to.

A decade later, when I interviewed several women who might have been the sisters of my mentors back in the early 1970s, I began to see their solitude, still an important feature of their lives, in a new way. Independence was now a demon these women struggled with. The early battles they'd fought to clear the way for women like me were still fresh in their minds from the days when, as the first women of the Control Generation, they set off with their backpacks and copies of Millett and Greer to test their independence. Now established as lawyers or professors or social workers in sunny apartments across the country, these Brave New Women reminded me that, until the 1970s, most urban landlords refused to rent apartments to single women, believing they must be prostitutes if they chose to live alone. When a woman looked for work in the HELP WANTED sections of big city newspapers, she found professional openings listed in "male only" columns. If she talked her way into an interview, employers freely asked whether she planned to marry, even whether she was using birth control. (In most cases the answer to this last question would have been no since, in the early 1970s, unmarried women in most states still had to lie to get birth control prescriptions. Ironically, sleeping around was safer for married women.)

A Brave New Woman never expected to combat such widespread discrimination on her own. But, while she might have joined forces with other women in consciousness-raising groups or feminist cells, her closest companions in those days were ideas, not people. To the Brave New Woman, dependence on a man was taboo, and even her supportive women friends were struggling with the same problems. As long as she had no role models, professionalism, feminism, and sexual liberation—the three pillars of the Myth of Independence—were a woman's only guides when she pioneered in offices, professional schools and between the sheets.

All of the women I interviewed had been touched by these movements, but the Brave New Women were positively driven by them. Looking for replacements for the housewife role, Ellen Barnes the Professional, Lynn Feldman the Feminist, and Rikki Sanchez the Sexual Revolutionary reached out to causes for their new identities. Yet once established in careers and fully independent in heart, mind and body, these defiantly self-directed women were left without the companionship of ideas. Even for the most dedicated women, the costs of independence and political purity outstripped the benefits. Their victories were behind them, and Brave New Women found themselves, now that they felt ready for love and even marriage, estranged from their own feelings and unable to cope with others'. Learning to stand up for themselves had meant shutting off woman's once instinctive emotionality and compassion. The same skills the Professional, the Feminist and the Sexual Revolutionary had learned in order to survive in her Brave New World were also defenses against closeness. The Brave New Woman was left alone with a special fear: that if she compromised her ideas by falling in love, her newfound self would be lost. As a result her life, once a glory of choices, seemed reduced to a single insoluble dilemma. Or at least that's the way it looked for Ellen Barnes.

1 § The Professional: Ellen Barnes

"To people at work I come off like I can handle anything, and that I'm tough and nobody can get to me. That's what you have to portray at work, but how do you turn it off at five or seven or ten o'clock and become a different person?"

A Show of Force

"Come on up!"—the words echoed down from the fourth-floor landing as I climbed the stairs of the Upper West Side brownstone to meet attorney Ellen Barnes. We'd talked several times on her office phone—Ellen spends so much time at work she'd told me not even to bother trying to reach her at home—and the familiar firm tones of the voice beckoning me up were so unmistakably lawyerly, I half expected to find a dark-suited woman with a briefcase waiting for me as I turned up the last flight.

Ellen Barnes was dressed instead in worn jeans and a snug yellow Lacoste T-shirt, but she still radiated professional competence. A fine-boned yet athletic woman with sharp dark eyes and a cap of raven-black hair, she turned on a smile so full of confidence it seemed almost to pump into me as we shook hands. Ellen, I already knew, had made a name for herself in her profession, rising swiftly in a prestigious Manhattan law firm until at twenty-nine she had become the highest-ranking woman in what had once been a male bastion—and immediately I understood why. This sleek woman with the flashing, intelligent eyes, would make a place for herself anywhere, and then make her presence felt.

The front door of Ellen's apartment opened onto a small space that looked bigger for its spare furnishings: a simple linen couch and a pair of matching chairs made up the living room, and a ladderlike set of stairs led up to a sleeping loft with picture windows so enormous they lit up both rooms. Like many of the apartments I'd visited, Ellen's felt more like a launching pad than a resting place. We sat on the couch, Ellen nestled in one corner with her legs tucked balletically beneath her as if ready to spring—indeed she often jumped up during the interview to make tea or answer the phone. This pose, as if always on the brink of action, seemed natural in Ellen Barnes, who describes herself as "a doing kind of person."

But as Ellen talked on, describing the conflicts between love and work that had dominated her life for nearly a decade, another woman seemed to emerge, ready, at last, to declare the conflict unbearable. This Ellen, a quieter but equally passionate woman, admitted she was tired of fitting her emotional life into late-night phone calls with women friends and visits to an out-of-town lover on alternate weekends. She was beginning to question the value of the professional pose that carried her safely through her days, but left her lonely at night. It was this Ellen who told me, suddenly tearful, about confronting what she called "the all-time big decision: commitment to a career or commitment to a relationship." It was the same terrible choice I was hearing about from successful women in cities from New York to San Francisco, a choice that was virtually inevitable for the single professional woman who sought success while ignoring her private life. The pieces of Ellen's life, as she entered her thirties, weren't fitting together. In fact, they were tearing her apart.

Learning to Be Hard

When Ellen Barnes entered law school in 1972, just 4 percent of the nation's lawyers and judges were women. Even more than medicine, where women had long accounted for a small but active 10 percent of the country's physicians, the law was male territory. During the decade in which she earned her degree and began practicing law, the number of female lawyers more than tripled; by 1980 a third of all law students were women. But the front line of female attorneys like Ellen were, often as not, unwelcome guests in the fraternity. As Ellen says, "No one was giving us any clues—we had to find it all out by trial and error. And when we started out, we were all thinking a lot more about the trials than the errors."

Like most career women of her generation, Ellen's decision to become a lawyer was more personal than political. Yet, as for most successful women, this was to be the last personal decision of her career. The fledgling attorney had joined a movement that would shape her life more than any personal inclination. She would have to struggle for her place in a man's world that did not welcome individuality. And the most obvious sign of her difference was, of course, her sex. To succeed she would have to conform to habits of dress, manners, even of thinking, established centuries ago by men: she would become, above all else, a Professional.

For Ellen Barnes, the early years were easier than for most. She was recruited by a progressive law firm in New York City eager to hire the new women coming out of law schools. She had no tales to match those of the Houston lawyer who had been greeted at her first board meeting by a conference room full of male colleagues tossing a condom around the table. Nor did she, as an Atlanta lawyer reported, have to enter the courtroom to argue her first case only to be asked by the judge why her boss had sent his secretary. But no professional woman in the mid-1970s could escape the burden of proving herself. Even if her reasons for coming to work were unique, she was viewed by male bosses and co-workers as a representative of what all women could—and couldn't—do. Like many women breaking into the professions, Ellen felt she had to perform even better than her male colleagues because she was so closely watched, and because, as a test case, the fate of future women in the firm depended on her. Yet to all the women who stayed on the job through the early years of catcalls and pranks, the working world was as challenging as it was threatening. The Professional often enjoyed proving herself even more than she liked doing her job.

Proving oneself was always more than half the battle. Most women drawn into the professions in the early 1970s knew the business world only as a far-off territory of personal freedom and material reward that fathers and uncles and brothers traveled to but rarely mentioned to young girls. Their rare glimpses of that world of apparent privilege often fired a desire to reach it, even as they left women sadly unprepared for the journey. The Professional often felt closer to her mother, but closeness was not part of that world she wanted to inhabit: she wanted, instead, her distant father's freedom.

Many Professionals considered their housewife mothers failures because they had staked their lives on relationships with husbands and children, never developing the skills to operate in the impersonal male world of merit. Even if their mothers' marriages were still intact (and many Professionals were the daughters of embittered divorcées), most of the successful women I interviewed saw their mothers suffer in middle age from loneliness and low self-esteem. Where her mother was left alone and helpless in middle age, the Professional would harden herself against such a fate, learning instead to thrive on her own. A career in the law—or medicine, or business—was, for the Professional, the most attractive escape from a life that she could only imagine ending in desertion, if not by her husband then certainly by the children who would otherwise become the focus of her adult years.

Attracted as much to the mannerisms of success as to success itself, the Professional often attempted to outperform her male colleagues not just in work, but in the Professional code of behavior. This meant dressing in subdued clothing, stifling her emotional responses, canceling lunch and dinner appointments to work overtime, traveling frequently, and even moving to another city when employers demanded it. Relationships with anyone outside work became handicaps: throughout the 1970s, singleness was the price most women paid for success. Studies of women's earnings showed that single women in every profession far surpassed married women, and received greater respect from male colleagues—most of whom were married. Marriage allowed ambitious men an autonomy that women could achieve only if they were single. Eventually the round-the-clock lives of these highly motivated women became so harried, many complained, humorously, that what they really needed was a wife.

But that was as far as the Professional's appreciation of the housewife went. Rejecting the plump, happy mother image to become the single woman in tweeds, she didn't want any of the nagging concerns or burdensome sympathies of the housewife. Emotion—the lack of control it brought, and the responsibility to others it so often required—was her chief enemy. In her job, the Professional believed, she would learn to control her feelings in a way her housewife mother, dependent on the love of others, had never managed. The impersonal atmosphere of the office was in many ways a refuge to this generation of women who had viewed firsthand in their mothers the disastrous effects of a life based solely on nurturing.

Still, for most professional women, there would come a time when control was too costly to maintain, when, as one recent business school graduate said, "I realized you can't be a professional *and* a woman—and suddenly I wanted to be more of a woman." The escape from feeling and from intimacy was bound to lead the Professional into a crisis later in life: a crisis like the one Ellen Barnes was confronting when at last, at twenty-nine, those emotions came spilling forth. Here's how it happened to Ellen.

Making All the Right Decisions

Looking back on her life, Ellen Barnes attributes many of her current troubles to having been a natural achiever. And achieve she did. During high school in a suburb north of

Boston, Ellen's classmates voted her cheerleader and class treasurer in both her junior and senior years. A much-dated "smart" girl who could turn on charm, wit, or determination as the occasion demanded, Ellen learned rules easily and loved to play by them. She nearly always won.

On scholarship at Boston University, she met Jim Reid in the fall of 1970, their junior year, and knew at once that she'd met her man. In the unsettled atmosphere of student revolt, Jim had plans for the future. His ambition was to become a lawyer, a dream he'd had ever since helping out in the family firm as a boy. Both Ellen and Jim still believed in true love and commitment, even marriage. They shared Ellen's dorm room that fall, and moved into an apartment for the spring semester. But they planned to live together only until graduation—marriage was their ultimate goal.

Raised by parents who had encouraged her only to "do well" at whatever she chose, Ellen herself wasn't sure what, besides marriage, she wanted to do well *at*. She'd considered social work or graduate school in her major, history, but as she grew closer to Jim and the two began to talk seriously about a wedding, she felt drawn to a more rigorous career as a kind of mooring in the perilous marital waters. "I don't know where I picked up the idea," Ellen says, "but I instinctively felt a need to be anchored in the outside world. I didn't want to depend on Jim for everything. I didn't think that would be fair to Jim, and I didn't like the thought of what it would do to me. Besides, I was used to doing well at things—I didn't want to stop." When Jim suggested law school, Ellen took to the idea immediately. Law school would challenge her academically. Better still, Ellen liked to think of the two of them attending classes and studying together and then, like Katharine Hepburn and Spencer Tracy in *Adam's Rib*, moving on to demanding careers in different legal specialties. Whenever she thought of their life together, Ellen imagined two graceful racehorses at the front of the pack, always running neck and neck. They announced their engagement in June; that same month they took the law boards together.

"Everything was going along fine," says Ellen, "until the

day our law board scores came in the mail. I scored a full hundred points higher on the test than Jim did: something we'd just never expected." With competition stiff, the couple knew that Ellen's high grades and scores meant their chances of ending up at the same law school were slim. Ellen and Jim applied to dozens of law schools in cities where there were more than one to choose from. Something would work out, they were sure. But nothing could change the fact that Ellen had outshone her fiancé at his life's ambition.

If it had all happened ten years earlier, Ellen might have deferred to Jim, dropping out of the running for law school admission entirely. Ellen knew plenty of women her mother's age who'd done that. Her own mother had given up a promising career in real estate when she began out-earning Ellen's father. "She started working when I was in high school," Ellen says. "She'd dropped out of college to marry my father, so real estate was about the only job with a future in it. She's a very spunky lady and turned out to be a great salesman. But when she started pulling in high commissions, my father put his foot down and said we didn't need the money. She quit working and now she's taking courses at the community college, but she's not really happy. She feels she had to choose between her marriage and doing the work that made her feel capable and successful. She ended up feeling suffocated and bitter, with all that energy turned inward, against herself. That's why, when the test scores came back, I felt I'd better worry about me. I didn't want to end up frustrated because there were so many should-have-beens and should-have-dones." Ellen sent off her applications and tried hard to believe Jim's halfhearted assurances that he was proud to have a fiancée who could beat him at his own game. It wasn't her fault, Ellen told herself, that she had studied hard and tested better. Jim would have to accept it—she wasn't going to turn away from success.

The following April, when the couple were mailing invitations to their June wedding, the mailbox failed them again. Ellen's envelopes were all fat acceptances, while

Jim's were all thin rejections. "We talked about putting off the marriage, things were that tense," Ellen recalls, "but our plans had been set for so long there just didn't seem to be any way to reverse them. At the time I didn't question things like that. When we were in college, getting engaged was the right thing to do. And the next logical step was to get married. I wanted to go through with it—I was proud of making all the right decisions. But I was going to have more. I was going to go on to law school and I was going to be a lawyer. I realize now that year was the beginning of the end, but at the time I just thought I was doing all the right things at the right time, and it never occurred to me that I would run into trouble."

The next fall, the two lived in the same student apartment in Boston as husband and wife, with Ellen attending Harvard Law School, and Jim working construction during the day while cramming for the law boards again at night. It was a delicate arrangement, one that would set the tone for their marriage now that Ellen had pulled into the lead. "It was hard to feel good about myself," Ellen recalls, "when I felt inside that I was taking something away from Jim. As much as I believed that women should be able to do whatever they want, it was incredibly destructive to our relationship that I was doing better at what had been Jim's lifelong dream—and I had only decided to apply to law school because he suggested it. The whole first year, I only studied when Jim was out of the house. I tried to pretend that I wasn't even going to school. But all day in classes, I was trying to pretend I wasn't married. Not that I was sleeping around, but most of the women at school were single and putting their whole lives into their work. No one was slacking off because they had to go home and cook dinner or spend time with their husbands. I felt I had to come off as just as independent as they were. It was part of learning to be a lawyer."

Well aware of Ellen's fears of a defeat like her mother's, Jim knew better than to bring up her increasing careerism for discussion. Instead, as the gap between Ellen's professional and personal commitments widened, Jim resorted to petty jealousies. Although Ellen tried to keep her work undercover, she recalls, "Jim was jealous of the men in my study group. He'd always accuse me of spending more time with them than I had to. He had no sympathy for how hard it was to be the only woman in a lot of situations. He just saw that as a chance for me to be unfaithful to him. Looking back on it, I realize he was jealous that I had a life separate from his which was exactly the life he wanted for himself. I didn't see it this way at the time, but our arguments were very much like the ones my parents had before my mother quit her job—except with the roles reversed. *She* didn't want to be missing out on the freedom my father had."

But Ellen and Jim hung on until the following year when Jim managed to pull up his law board scores enough to get into law school at B.U. The two lived out an approximation of their original dream for the next two years: Jim excelled in courtroom competitions, Ellen made law review, and they felt for the first time in their marriage equally matched. But both of them knew that soon enough Ellen would graduate ahead of Jim, Ellen would get the first job, and with her Harvard degree it would probably be a better job than Jim would ever find.

When an offer came in from a prestigious Manhattan law firm, Ellen accepted it, hoping to spend the year alone in New York and commute on weekends until Jim could join her in the city on a more equal footing. But Jim, fearful that the separation would only put new strains on an already faltering marriage, insisted on transferring to a New York law school for his final year. The move took him away from the friends and activities he had cultivated in Boston, and left him more of a househusband than ever before. Ellen and Jim went back to living out the same unwanted experiment in sex-role reversal.

Given the chance to prove herself in a demanding job, Ellen gave up all efforts to limit her working hours. "I never felt the pressure that everybody talks about in the early years at a big firm," Ellen recalls of her first year in New York, "but the job fostered my tendency to be a work-aholic. There was always too much work to do, and be-

cause I am a perfectionist at heart I could never let any of it
slide. Besides, those were the rules everyone played by:
you just stayed as long as it took for you to do the best
possible job.

"It wasn't long before the trouble started. Every afternoon at about five-thirty my phone would ring and it would
be Jim saying, 'I've been home for an hour or two. What
time do you think you'll be home tonight?' I used to just
dread that phone call every single night because I felt so
guilty. All I could say was, 'Well, probably seven or eight,
but I'm not sure, I'll call you later.' Then if I got tied up
and didn't have a chance to call, he'd call again with,
'Where the hell *are* you? What have you been doing? I can't
believe you have really been working all this time.' As if I'd
deliberately waste time around the office so I couldn't go
home! I wanted to be home as much as he wanted me to be
there.

"Jim was home every afternoon at two or three, and since
his grades didn't matter by the second semester, he didn't
have all that much to do except to resent me. After a while
he just refused to pick up the cleaning, or do the laundry or
the shopping, so on my one day off I shopped and went to
the dry cleaners and took care of all the things that he didn't
do during the week out of spite. I could understand that he
wasn't getting what he wanted out of life and out of our
relationship. He was feeling very needy and I wasn't there
to help him. But I was feeling very needy too, by the time I
got home at ten or eleven o'clock after riding the subway,
and I really wasn't able to give him anything. All I could do
was eat and sleep, and get up the next morning and take the
train back to work and start in all over again. A lot of the
time I was just as angry and frustrated about the demands
of my job as Jim was, but I wasn't getting any support from
him. I was being pulled in two different directions, and I
just couldn't stand it.

"It got to the point where I was responsible not only for
all the housework, but for the finances too. Whenever
things got tight, which was pretty often because we were
paying off loans and living in the most expensive city in the

country, Jim would panic and keep asking over and over, 'What are we going to do, what are we going to do?' *I* had to figure a way out, *I* was the one who had to say, 'Look, we'll make it. There's a paycheck coming in.' When I finally walked out, I was beyond feeling hurt or loss—I just wanted somebody to take care of *me* for a change."

Sadly, in cultivating a strength and independence based on gradually shutting off the wifely sympathy that she believed would prevent her from realizing her potential as a lawyer, Ellen had shut herself out of a relationship that might have supported her through the difficult first years on the job. Since entering law school she had been making all the right decisions for Ellen Barnes, the Professional. But what about Ellen Barnes, the woman?

The Mistaken Choice: Me or the Marriage

Like many of the women I interviewed, Ellen Barnes was living by the Myth of Independence at the same time as she was reacting to what she saw as the central failures of her mother's life. The combination proved impossible. Like her mother, Ellen had formed a close relationship with a man while still in college, and she had married him. But unlike her mother, she would not quit school, nor back off from her career even when it directly threatened her husband. For Ellen, her job occupied the emotional center of her life.

"I wanted more, I was going to go on to law school and be a lawyer," Ellen had said. And for Ellen, as for most career women of her generation, *being* a lawyer meant just that, an almost complete merging of identity and occupation. Says Ellen, "I don't think women today go into careers for the same reasons men do. We don't do it because Daddy said so or because we're saving to buy a house and support a family. I didn't grow up knowing I would go into law or medicine or anything else. But once I started working it was even more important to me than if I had planned for it my whole life, because the whole reason I was doing it was for *me*, for *my* satisfaction, and to show that I could do something women had never done before. It became more than a job. It became part of my identity." With her mother's bleak example in mind, it was a part of her identity Ellen would protect even at the cost of her marriage.

Even if she had been able to make time for love, there was something about the way she pursued her career that had made her less loving, and less lovable. "Let's face it," Ellen told me, "law is still a man's business. As a woman you have to be very careful. Women have to compensate, we cannot be weak, we cannot be emotional. In a lot of ways men can get away with showing more emotion. When a man in the office gets angry he can slam his fist on the desk and it's perfectly acceptable. Nobody says he is being irrational or overreacting, no one calls him an 'emotional woman.'"

Worse, just when she most needed emotional support, Ellen had to avoid all emotional ties, thereby continuing the pattern she had set out of peer pressure in law school. "As a woman you have to appear unattached," Ellen continues. "I could never say I had to spend more time at home with my husband. It would have sounded like I couldn't stand up to any man if I couldn't say no to my husband. One of the male attorneys could go in and say his wife is bitching that he's not home enough, and get some time off. That's his way of asking. The partners understand, they've been through it themselves." Although she understood that it was "incredibly destructive" to her marriage that she was so thoroughly occupied with the profession that had been Jim's lifelong dream, it was an understanding that Ellen could not afford to act on or even to think about.

The price of success was monitoring her emotions, an act that Ellen, like most women new to the professions, had trouble dropping after hours. "To people at work I come off like I can handle anything, and that I'm tough and nobody can get to me," Ellen says. "That's what you have to portray at work, but how do you turn it off at five or seven or ten o'clock and become a different person? You get to feeling that you are always on, and it's hard to let that feeling go, because when you shut it off, you're vulnerable."

Ellen had entered so deeply into the professional role that

she felt she would have to "become a different person" in
order to escape it for just a few hours. The law was no
longer just a part of her identity; it had taken over entirely.
"I keep thinking back now to the arguments Jim and I used
to have when we were splitting up," Ellen says. "Not so
much what we argued about, but how Jim used to look at
me and say, 'You're talking like a lawyer now. Don't talk to
me like a lawyer.'" At the time the remark infuriated her;
she felt Jim was threatened by her newfound strength. But
Ellen never dropped the facade long enough to find out.
Ellen Barnes had become the Professional, a lawyer
twenty-four hours a day. As she says, "I let the rationality
of law interfere with purely emotional decisions. I don't
think I was even capable of making a purely emotional
decision anymore, of getting down to what *I felt*."

Ellen may have developed a stronger sense of self by
learning to perform in the male legal world, but, ironically,
it was a self that didn't allow for feelings. Like many
women eager to attain the competence that confinement to
the traditional female roles of wife and mother had denied
to earlier generations, Ellen had accepted wholeheartedly
the impersonal standards of the workplace. She had learned
to win in a world where what she *did* mattered more than
what she *felt*. Strangely, this woman who easily asserted
herself at work feared being vulnerable at home and could
not ask that her emotional needs be met. Often she was not
even aware of them. Ellen reached the climactic final year
of her marriage wishing, more than anything, to be taken
care of. She had made the mistake of believing in the corporate definition of strength: never to acknowledge feeling.
She found out later that her feelings were still there, but by
that time she could only look elsewhere for someone to
confide in.

Getting Emotional

Ellen's emotions found their outlet soon enough in what
seems in retrospect like the only logical place: an office
romance. When she fell in love with David Matthews, an-

other lawyer at the firm who was also ending a rocky marriage, Ellen discovered the perfect solution to her tightly controlled life. For one thing, David loved her for the professional image that caused Jim so much anxiety. "I was happy for the first time in a really long time," Ellen recalls. "We worked together, we respected each other very much as lawyers. He understood everything I was going through at the office because he was going through similar things with the same people. It was so easy to talk about things. He was very, very supportive, and my work never seemed like a threat to him. Life was really terrific. At the start there were lots of great times where we'd be at work with the same pressures and demands, and then we could both walk off the job—even at ten o'clock at night—and go have a drink and dinner and relax and unwind together. We were both on the same wave length." At last Ellen was living her dream of an equal partnership in love.

For a time, Ellen even seemed to be loosening up, given the chance to be more emotional on the job. "It was nice knowing that there was somebody you could just pop in on or call on the phone because he was right there," Ellen says. "There were times when things would get bad at work or at home, and I could just go upstairs to his office and close the door and I could cry there, and get the support I needed to get over whatever turmoil I was going through. It was the first time in a long time I'd felt safe letting my feelings out. It was really positive—both professionally and personally." Although Ellen and David hid their love affair in their private offices and the one-bedroom apartment Ellen had recently rented, she was beginning to open up.

But inevitably, Ellen's old fear of an emotional dependence resurfaced. Both Ellen and David had initiated divorce proceedings, but neither one felt prepared for another wedding just yet. Much as she felt she loved David, she was not eager to enter the kind of dependent relationship that had caused her so much trouble with Jim. Plus, Ellen had begun to feel that having someone in the office know just how easy it had been for her to go to pieces was undermining her work. David had come a little too close for comfort.

When a sympathetic partner in the firm, whom both Ellen and David confided in, warned that one of them would have to leave the firm eventually, whether or not the affair turned to marriage, it seemed like a blessing in disguise. David had connections with a Washington, D.C., firm and had long hoped to move down to work for the federal government. A few phone calls produced an offer. Ellen suggested he take the job; she would quit hers and follow him south after finishing an important case in New York. Even if they were separated for the several months it might take for Ellen to find work in Washington, the distance might help heal old wounds from previous marriages and allow the two of them to build up separate lives.

Ellen's case dragged on long past the few months of separation the two expected, and Ellen herself began to thrive on her work in a way she never had before. The combination of the years she'd put in on the job, and the security of David's love, safe and undemanding in Washington, with no guilt-provoking phone calls at five-thirty every day, brought out the best in her. She no longer had to hide her affair, but neither did it interfere with her work. And on the salaries of two corporate lawyers it was easy to shuttle between the two cities on alternate weekends, even if Ellen was carrying heavy briefcases from work along with her overnight bag.

"I'd have to admit," Ellen says, "that a long-distance relationship fit a pattern that I felt comfortable with. I think women have a much harder time than men making the transition from work to home—it's a farther distance for them to travel. Life was easier for me separated into parcels: *my* life, *our* life, weekdays and weekends." For Ellen, a long-distance affair was a way of having it all on her own terms. The arrangement wasn't always an easy one. "I was three different people," Ellen says. "I was work, I was the life I had found for myself Monday through Friday here with my friends. And then, David and I had to crowd an entire week's worth of relationship into a weekend." Yet most of the time being three different people was easier than trying to be all three at once.

Ellen had at last become the woman in tweeds, the single independent Professional whose love affairs were subordinate to her work—and whose image she had aspired to even in her marriage. The long-distance affair allowed Ellen to get away with the polarization of work and love commitments that had plagued her marriage yet seemed important in protecting her emerging identity. Ellen continued to promise David she would look for work in Washington as soon as her case concluded, but as the time drew nearer, she began to worry. "I'd gotten used to the feeling of being in control of my life," says Ellen. "Part of it comes from living alone in the city. No one is there to make sure I get into my apartment and lock the doors behind me at night. I'm always on guard, and I have to be totally in control all the time. But I was also having a good time being my own boss, coming and going when I wanted to. The longer I stood on my own, the harder it was to start leaning on somebody else and have somebody else lean on me and share my life. I really wasn't sure I could do it." Ellen heard about friends who had left town to follow lovers, then grown dissatisfied with their new jobs and returned to New York alone and out of work. She thought more about her mother's decision to give up real estate, and knew she couldn't bear the bitterness. But she knew she loved David. The move to Washington wouldn't mean giving up—would it?

At a luncheon celebrating the close of Ellen's case, a senior partner took her aside to discuss her future with the firm. If she kept up the good work, he told Ellen, she'd be certain to make partner within two years. The firm needed a woman like her, a woman who wouldn't give in. Ellen didn't tell him that "giving in" was just what she'd been thinking of doing.

Back in Control

"So, after a year of commuting," Ellen explained, the tears forming in her dark eyes, "we hit the all-time big decision: commitment to a career or commitment to a relationship. There just was no good answer. Either David had to give up a good job where he would make partner in two years and his life in a new city that he likes more than New York, or I had to give up exactly the same things. There was no in-between. There was no compromise." Ellen looked for jobs on her weekends in Washington, sent letters of application, but the effort was halfhearted. "I kept asking myself, 'What about me and everything I've worked for?' I was prepared to give up my job as long as I could find something good down there to take its place. But I didn't want to throw down the tubes four years of sweat and fighting to get where I was just to work at some small firm where they don't practice law the same way, and where my chances of partnership would be uncertain. At this point in my career, leaving town would almost guarantee never making partner."

Ellen had grown so accustomed to resisting David's pleas for her to move, so convinced that they were, like Jim's demands for her time, the appeals of a man determined to undermine her selfhood, that she was shocked the day, just a week before we met, when David called to tell her he had given up waiting. "He was gentle about it at first," Ellen says, the tears falling now, "but he was firm. He told me he knew I was never going to move, that my job meant too much to me, and we were fooling ourselves. That was it, an ultimatum." She pauses, then adds bitterly, "I didn't know why it happened so fast until I found out through friends that he'd been seeing another woman—a nursery school teacher of all things, when all that time he'd been telling me how much he admired me as a professional."

Ellen marvels now at how quickly she made a decision that had plagued her for over a year. "Normally, I'd have been in hysterics," says Ellen, back in control, "but instead I called him right back and said, very calmly, 'I want you too much to let you go.' He was too surprised to respond then, and he said he would take the weekend to think it over. Yesterday I sent him a registered letter saying I know that after all we've been through it's hard for him to believe I mean this, but I'd like to move down there, job or no job, if he'll let me, and just see how things work out. It felt good, it felt like for the first time I'd taken control of my personal life."

What made Ellen change her mind? Would she find a freer emotional life by "taking control," tossing aside certain partnership and throwing herself at the mercy of David? I asked Ellen what made her choice different from her mother's decision to drop real estate in order to save her marriage. "I think I've come to it after more experience of the working world," Ellen answers. "I realized something in the middle of all this. I have a great job, a wonderful apartment, enough money to be self-indulgent. You'd think my life was ideal! But you run and run and run and then you wake up one day and you're twenty-nine and a half and you say, 'What do I have to show for it?' There is not a damn thing I don't have—except the one thing I now know I want more than anything else, David. As much satisfaction as I get out of my job, it just doesn't keep me warm at night. It is not going to be enough for me to make partner two years from now and come home to an empty house."

As Ellen let me out of her apartment, once again the firm-voiced Professional I met at the head of the stairs, I told her I hoped David would accept her proposal: she seemed so much to want him. But as I thought later about Ellen's life, I began to wonder what her sudden decision really amounted to. Perhaps she was applying her business know-how to personal affairs, at last learning to serve her emotional needs as she had her career goals. But the prompt phone call, the registered letter, the satisfaction in finally taking control of her personal life, reminded me, too, of Ellen's inability to drop the professional pose in her marriage to Jim. Would it be a different Ellen who moved south to share her life with David? Or was Ellen simply striking the best deal she could, once the stakes were changed and she found herself competing with another woman for partnership in David's life?

I sensed that Ellen herself didn't know the answer. For even as she had struggled most of her life to avoid the terrible choice between love and work her mother had faced, she had moved inexorably toward it by taking the opposite course. She had based her self-worth almost solely on work and encouraged David to do the same. Just when he was growing closest to her, she suggested he leave town to build up a separate life—one that could only lead to their estrangement. Ellen put off her choice so long that in the end it was forced on her—just as her mother's had been. Ellen *was* capable of managing her personal life: she had at last acknowledged the depth of her emotions. But this decision, which quite likely would overwhelm David with its suddenness, seemed unlikely to end the conflict between the opposing loyalties to work and to love that raged within Ellen Barnes.

While many professional women have learned a new competence and self-respect on the job, they have not yet resolved the split between love and work they inherited from their housewife mothers. Like Ellen, they have never learned to set reasonable boundaries on love relationships, only to set limits on their own emotions. Love still seems an all-or-nothing proposition that, given their newfound self-sufficiency, seems hardly worth the high investment.

Love is always a perilous adventure. In the past, for women it was also their only security, their only livelihood. Many women sought love with a nearly obsessive spirit. Now jobs provide the security that love once did, and many women have allowed their work to consume them, taking the place of long-term love. With work taking over the center of her life, love became, for the Professional, an unnecessary risk. It would become an even greater threat to the Feminist, whose work itself plays out her profound distrust of men.

2 § The Feminist: Lynn Feldman

"It's one thing to have a room of one's own—but can you live your whole life in it?"

Sisterhood Is Powerful

Jobs, day-care centers, birth control pills, women's sports, separate checking accounts, pants—all these things could be found before 1970. But now they are in profusion everywhere. Women take them for granted; so do men. Far more sweeping than the employment revolution, the women's movement invaded all aspects of traditional female life—and changed most of them.

In 1971, in the first issue of *Ms.* magazine, Jane O'Reilly wrote in her famous article, "The Housewife's Moment of Truth": "We have suddenly and shockingly perceived the basic disorder in what has been believed to be the natural order of things." Feminists were determined to challenge standard notions of woman's place in everything from government to the family. Sociologist Jessie Bernard told women just how far-reaching the movement would be in her book published the same year, *Women and the Public Interest.* "This revolution," she wrote, "is the most universal, most humane, and most human revolution of all. Who can be opposed to a revolution that asks, 'How do we live with others? How do we bring up our kids? How is family life and work shared? How can we all be human?'"

Yet the early questioners found that, particularly when it came to altering family dynamics, much of the rest of the world—their lovers, their husbands and children—wasn't so eager to change. The consciousness-raising-group divorce became almost a cliché, of which Betty Friedan's failed marriage was only the most famous example. In the late 1970s, Jessie Bernard wrote about the deterioration of her own marriage in *Self-Portrait of a Family*, news that was hardly surprising after her earlier condemnation of the institution in *The Future of Marriage*. Strained by these highest of ideals, the old ties would not hold.

The optimism of the early feminists gave way to an anger and militance that would forever mark its adherents' personal lives. "Women . . . must reject any revival of the romantic trap," wrote Rosemary Ruether in 1975 in *New Woman New Earth*, expressing the widespread belief that any intimate connection with men led women into dependence and compromise. Ti-Grace Atkinson, always an extremist, nevertheless touched the deeper suspicions of many women with her much quoted formula, "Love is the victim's response to the rapist." Simone de Beauvoir and Gloria Steinem never married. Adrienne Rich, Andrea Dworkin, Jill Johnston and Kate Millett advertised their political lesbianism: women were the only deserving objects of a woman's love. What began as the most human of movements ended as a movement of separatists.

By 1981, of the forty women I interviewed, all of whom were living lives that would have been inconceivable before the women's movement, only five identified themselves as feminists. And even these women, while crediting the movement with many of their new freedoms, blamed feminism for an emotional emptiness they felt in their lives. "What the women's movement lacks is compassion," said one woman, "compassion for the women who still want some of the traditional things: love, security, family life. And most of all it lacks compassion for men. How can I love someone I'm angry at?"

Looking back on a decade of abandoned lovers and ambitions, a thirty-year-old community organizer told me, "I can't stress enough how all my decisions were based on politics. I gave up a career in journalism I had dreamed about since childhood to work for the movement. I gave up lovers when they demanded too much. I don't regret any of it. What I did was right for me at the time. But now I'm beginning to wonder what I have left." The personal and the political were hopelessly intertwined, and some women felt as lost in sexual politics as their mothers had been in marriage. "Sometimes I think we were shoehorned into feminism the way our mothers were shoehorned into the suburbs," said one thirty-four-year-old woman whose inability to stay with a man for more than a few months had sent her into psychotherapy. "I don't know what's real and what's posture for me anymore," echoed an attorney whose marriage broke up at the height of the revolution. "I knew inside all along that I wanted to be with somebody, but I always felt I wasn't supposed to be, that love was a weakness, and I would become dangerously dependent."

Like professionalism, feminism filled a vacuum in the lives of young women who had rejected the housewife role. Their cause supported them in their search for an identity separate from wife and mother. Yet, as with the Professional, this new ideology fostered a distrust of intimacy and of emotion, the staples of the abandoned housewife role. Even as it addressed women's problems, feminism left many of its followers ambivalent about womanhood itself. Lynn Feldman was no exception.

Resisting the Feminine Role

I met Lynn Feldman in her office, a small basement room in the centuries-old red brick history department building of an Ivy League university. At first the office appeared typical of a career academic: walls covered with announcements of conferences and lecture series, and shelves bulging with books. But on closer inspection, Lynn's underground workroom looked more like a revolutionary stronghold. Instead of ancient leather-bound tomes, her books were an assortment of hastily published volumes of the latest scholarship in women's studies. Drawings of angry female faces and clenched fists decorated the bright-colored conference fliers, and nearly all bore the legend at the bottom of the page: "Only women invited."

From her seat at a large oak desk in the center of the clutter, Lynn stood up and reached across papers and books to shake hands warmly. A tall, chestnut-haired woman with tortoiseshell glasses, Assistant Professor Feldman wore a deep blue fisherman's sweater and corduroy jeans. She seemed a little wary despite the casual attire, but that may have stemmed from the adversity she faced. Although she had earned a national reputation in women's history, there was little support for her work here, even though the university had recently turned co-ed. In every other room of this building, she told me, men sit behind the desks, overseeing the work of students, teaching assistants, and assistant professors like Lynn Feldman. Those men, Lynn continued, had been working to exclude her since the day she arrived.

When Lynn Feldman came here four years ago, she had hoped to play a larger role in the university. She points to a tailored tweed jacket hanging on a coatrack behind the door. "I keep that here to remind me how far I've come," she says with a touch of bitterness. "When I first took the job," she explains, "I used to wear tweed suits all the time. I tried to fit in, and it shouldn't have been hard, since I was just as serious and scholarly as any of the men here. I still am, though not many of my colleagues see it that way. But eventually I saw there was no point in dressing for success. No matter what I wore, they were going to see me as Woman—with a capital *W*—never as Lynn Feldman, never as a scholar, and certainly never as an equal. I finally decided I might as well dress the way I wanted, and I started teaching what I wanted, too. The women's studies movement is the only place I was able to find professional friendships. My only real colleagues are hundreds of miles away."

Fitting in was never easy for Lynn. All her life she

seemed instinctively to know that making all the "right" decisions about jobs, men and marriage, as attorney Ellen Barnes had, would not be right for her. Yet she never gave up hoping to find a community that would include her—and she has routinely been disappointed. It's been that way since she was eighteen.

That year Lynn Feldman packed up a few tweed skirts and simple sweaters, several boxes of her favorite books, and left her family's ranch-style house in the upper-class Jewish suburb of Highland Park, Illinois, for a room in one of Wellesley College's ivy-covered dormitories. It was September of 1966. Eager to escape the high school where her bookishness marked her as a misfit, Lynn looked forward to meeting women at college who shared her interests and her problems.

Wellesley was also her mother's college, but that was about the only thing she was pleased to inherit from her mother. A coolly competent volunteerist who served on countless local arts and charity boards yet ran her handsome Highland Park residence with military efficiency, Mrs. Feldman was not the most inspiring role model for Lynn. "My mother raised me along traditional female lines," she says. "Her message was: be smart but not too smart—don't threaten men with your ideas. I tried not to pay much attention. I just applied to Wellesley and waited till I could get out. It never occurred to me that my mother might have been right about the way the world works."

Lynn is still appalled at her parting scene with her mother at the Chicago airport. "On the way over in the car, she was very icy toward me," Lynn recalls. "My father wasn't even there—probably he was traveling on business. Finally she said to me, as we pulled up at O'Hare, 'Remember, Lynn, no man wants a wife who's better at what he does than he is.' I realized then, though she never said so, how much she had given up, what a price she had paid. Here I was thinking about a wonderful future in academics, and she saw it as a time to give up my ambitions and look for a man." It was the mid-1960s, and Lynn didn't then know any words with which to respond. She just remembers feeling let down. "Just when I needed support," Lynn says, "she didn't even take me seriously.

"It was always that way with my mother," Lynn goes on. "I knew deep inside she was glad when I was doing well at school, but at the same time it frightened her. She felt she had the same kind of intelligence I did, but where did it get her? To be the president of the women's symphony club. There was no real pleasure in that. Her mind was only a source of frustration to her. She always felt trapped, and without meaning to hurt me, she was trying to keep me down, to protect me from that kind of disappointment. At the time, it just made me angry at *her*. Now I blame Wellesley and Highland Park and my father and just about everyone else. But then it kept us apart." From that day on, Lynn stopped telling her mother about her ambitions, afraid she'd only laugh them down. Still, her mother's defeatist example would stay with her through the next two decades.

Lynn faced even ruder surprises at Wellesley. "I expected everybody to take each other seriously and talk about important ideas," Lynn recalls, "but instead I found the same empty social scene as in high school. My classmates were all tracking down men, and the unspoken message from most of the professors and the administration was that we were being trained to be nothing more than good wives." The only difference from high school was that the men Lynn met at mixers were interested in dating brainy women. "Even so, they were looking at you as wife material—would I be good company at a cocktail party? Would I boost his career? They looked at women through a smoke screen. I finally met some graduate students who at least talked to me about *ideas*, but of course they were getting on in their careers, and wanted a wife who would follow them across country and raise their kids. They had no sense of *my* needs, of *my* life."

Nevertheless, Lynn fell in love with one of them. Andy Warren was the first man she met who respected her intelligence and welcomed its flowering. He was an instructor in history at Wellesley and seemed destined for a brilliant career. His own brightness illuminated Lynn's when they began a slow courtship that consisted first of long learned discussions of the kind Lynn had always dreamed about. She slept with him, but she didn't intend to marry him. That marked her, once again, as an outsider. Lynn says, "I was very peculiar at Wellesley for not having an engagement ring or my china pattern picked out. The other women were sleeping with their boyfriends, but only after they'd got the ring. It was sickening." Lynn had seen what marriage had done to her mother; she felt that as a lover she could hold on to whatever it was her classmates were trading in for a diamond. When she moved in with Andy at the end of her senior year, it was partly to prove to herself that her mother was wrong: she wouldn't have to forfeit her ambitions to a man.

If anything, life with Andy was proving just the opposite. Andy encouraged Lynn to apply to graduate school in history, the subject she had been discovering under his tutelage. Andy himself signed a seven-year contract at Wellesley that spring, so the two would not have to worry about a move or a separation. In the fall, Lynn enrolled at a large university, just a few miles away. "Andy was such a comfort to me in those days," Lynn recalls. "He encouraged me in my work, and though there was always a bit of condescension—he was the mentor and I was the perpetual student—Andy also was an assurance that I was attractive and feminine, even if I didn't go along with the rest of the women at Wellesley. And I found out that I could fall in love, something I'd actually begun to doubt after so many years alone."

Anger Without End

But in the early 1970s, the relationship that had seemed both adventurous and reassuring began, as Lynn discovered feminism, to seem nearly as destructive to her spirit as a marriage. "The women's movement came along and changed everything," Lynn remembers. "At first it all seemed to be going on in downtown Boston with a bunch of crazy, angry man-hating women marching and making absurd demands. I couldn't understand where all their anger was coming from. I went to a few student rallies at the university, but all I heard was a lot of jargon that didn't seem to fit my case. I was used to being on the outside, and I'd never had much to do with other women. I thought it was their fault if they had gone along with all the feminine trappings of dependence. But in graduate school I was forced to see myself as a woman, not as an exception. I found out how little power women really have even once, like me, they'd decided it was OK to be different. And Andy, because he was older and thriving on the academic system, began to seem like the enemy—or at least a false security when I should have been out there struggling on my own."

Much as Lynn had complained about her man-hunting classmates at Wellesley, a women's college seemed like a feminist support group compared to graduate school. "As a woman, I was one of the real pioneers in the department," Lynn says. "The men hadn't worked out a way to deal with women yet. I felt like a walking identity crisis—for them as much as for me. On one side there were the professors who would have nothing to do with the few women who were in the graduate program: they would never invite single women to their houses, even if they were holding a class seminar. Then on the other side were the gropers—grad students mostly, and some professors, who just couldn't keep their hands off. One time I was pinched in the butt. Another guy cornered me in my office and put his arms around me. I just ran. And a third one came up behind me in the photocopy room and started rubbing his hands up and down my back. They all assumed they were God's gift to womankind, and it never occurred to them I wasn't interested—even when they knew I was living with Andy."

It took Lynn some time to react. "As a first-year grad student you're so vulnerable," Lynn says, "because you never know who's going to be on the committee that's going to vote on whether you can stay. The first year I just took it and was miserable. Andy was no help. He kept trying to figure out if I was inviting it. I suppose it was the sort of thing that went on when he was in graduate school, and it just seemed normal to him. So I let it all happen to me— and it made me furious inside. I had this tremendous anger building, deep down in my gut. But I did nothing about it.

"The second year, the pendulum swung the other way. All you had to do was say 'woman' to me and I had my fists up. That was when I started telling people to get their hands off. Then I got the 'you're oversensitive' label. By that time, though, I was part of the department, and I knew they needed me for the research I was doing. It made *them* look good to have this bright young woman historian around. I started meeting with the other women in the department for lunch every week—there were just six of us—and we discussed everything from how to handle the gropers to why women weren't talked about in the history courses we were taking. It was a vital time for all of us, and our research and our ideas really started to expand. The whole field of women's studies was opening up, and we were all ecstatic to discover we could be feminists without resorting to the kind of jargon that I heard at the more radical demonstrations. We weren't man-haters; we were researching women's lives."

But as Lynn's position within her women's group and as a feminist historian became more secure, the less certain she was of her place in Andy's life. By the end of three years of graduate school, Andy and Lynn had grown apart. Lynn believed her research on the untold history of women was ground-breaking; Andy found it trivial. Now in his thirties, Andy had begun to talk about marriage and raising children. Lynn, however, was horrified. She had been study-ing the marriage contracts of the nineteenth century that deprived women of their names, property and right to their children, all for a ring—a thrall. More than ever, she de-spised the institution Andy was asking her to enter. Discus-sions of their relationship became debates about the course of American history.

Yet at her women's lunches, Lynn began to feel in-

creasingly defensive, for the opposite reason—for being the
one woman with a man. She felt that her Wellesley good-
girl past showed every time she slipped and mentioned
Andy's ideas on a subject, or skipped an important
women's history lecture to stay home. She began to feel
troubled that she had never lived by herself. She worried
even more that she often thought of herself in terms of a
couple: as "we" and not as "I." Was she losing herself to the
relationship? She began to fight her way out.

"I loved Andy," Lynn recalls, "but it began to seem that
we had very little in common. Even though we were both
in the same field, his attitude toward history was so different from mine. I couldn't make him understand my
point of view—and I think I had so much anger built up
toward the men in graduate school, and from what I was
finding out in my research, that I actually expected him to
turn around and tell me I was right and start apologizing for
the whole male race. Instead he was asking me to marry
him!"

The women's movement took shape at a time when
women like Lynn were still uncertain about the course of
their lives. Lynn had managed to reject the trappings of the
traditional female, yet she was still living with a man and
deriving a good deal of her self-assurance from him. She
had not yet found her separate identity. Feminism encouraged her to look for it. Yet the movement undermined the
one relationship that had so far helped her feel better about
herself and her place in the world. The feminism Lynn
learned from the women who were her new friends, and
that was fueled by the anger growing inside her, decreed
that women must find themselves *by* themselves. Feminism
ignored the fact that developing a capacity for intimacy is
one of the keys to growing up. "I had to know that I could
be a whole person before I married anyone," Lynn explains. "For me that was by proving to myself I could be
totally independent and totally in control of my life. I
didn't think it was possible to do that in a marriage. I didn't
believe it was possible to be close and set limits at the same
time, to say this is where I begin and you end. I just

thought I would disappear as a person. I know that's what happened to my mother."

Ambivalent about what were the most natural of desires—for love and security—Lynn, like many women, came to distrust the man who evoked these feelings in her. Andy's talk of marriage seemed to have nothing to do with her own best interests; instead it seemed to be part of the masculine conspiracy to keep women down. The central feminist precept, that woman's institutionalized dependence on men prevented her from realizing her own powers, pointed the Feminist in only one direction: isolation. Unlike the Professional, whose aim was to become one of the guys, the Feminist was prepared to slam the door on all of them.

With her dissertation nearly complete, Lynn applied for teaching positions at several universities outside the state, hoping for an excuse to break with Andy. When an offer came through from an Ivy League university in the process of going co-ed, Lynn accepted without a second thought. "It was hard telling Andy I had to leave," she recalls, "but if I married Andy, I thought Lynn Feldman was going to be obliterated."

Woman as Victim

Like the other feminists I interviewed, Lynn Feldman's rage was fueled by wrongs done to two women: herself and her mother. If Lynn's mother had conveyed any satisfaction in the housewife role, Lynn might not have been so determined to reject the "trappings of femininity," nor so bitter about the struggles she faced. Instead, Lynn was carrying with her the awareness of her mother's "obliteration" as well as the fear of her own undoing.

The feminists I talked to had come nowhere near being housewives. Their every step after leaving home took them away from the kitchen. As one woman said, "I was so angry, I refused to do any of the expected womanly things. I wouldn't so much as boil a pot of water for a man." Still, these women labored under the unexpressed anger of gen-

erations of housewives. Their own mothers and grandmothers had rarely complained about their losses. Instead
the daughters had to guess at their pain in scenes like the
airport parting Lynn described, where mothers tried to
stand in the way of their daughters' cherished ambitions for
independence. The daughter then suffered two losses: she
lost her mother's sympathy and her example as a role
model. For some, as with Lynn, there were initial periods
of anger with their mothers for holding their daughters
back. Yet inevitably, perhaps in order to save themselves
from perpetual anger toward their closest parent, it became
easier to blame men: fathers, brothers and grandfathers,
and the male-dominated society at large. Feminism gave
women a way of sympathizing with their mothers while
allowing them to stand up for themselves.

But unfortunately Lynn's new beliefs were essentially
negative. For much as feminism sought to promote the
cause of women, it was based on a view of women as victim. The Feminist could find only the slightest dignity in
the women of older generations, and that was the dignity of
martyrs. Each new wrong she spotted, in the workplace, in
the home, in society, reinforced the view, already learned
from her mother's example, that women were easily exploited. Like the Professional, then, the Feminist came to
view her own gender as a liability. But in the Feminist's
view femininity wasn't simply an impediment to success—
it doomed her.

Like the Professional, the Feminist refused to accept an
adult identity defined by marriage and motherhood. She
believed, as in her mother's case, that motherhood was the
opposite: a suppression of self. The Professional often
blamed her mother for failing to realize her potential for
meaningful work outside the home. Yet Ellen Barnes had at
least seen signs of life in her mother: Mrs. Barnes was
strong enough to take the blame for not making more of
herself. Ellen believed the battle for a place in a man's
world was one she could win if she simply avoided making
her mother's mistakes. Cool, aloof, and not even much of a

mother, Mrs. Feldman seemed to her historian daughter
the casualty of a war lost centuries ago.

In self-defense, Lynn resisted all that was traditionally
feminine. She rejected her mother's advice, the fear-of-
success doctrine; she avoided the seductive games her classmates played, or participated unhappily. "I always felt as if
I were in drag," Lynn recalled of her attempts at dating, "a
female impersonator in my heels and makeup and earrings,
trying to be a good listener to some self-important jerk."
She avoided romantic involvements unless she could play
them out in a significantly new way. Living with Andy
worked for a while. But when the women's movement came
along to support Lynn in her rejection of the feminine role,
even cohabitation, a gesture of rebellion a few years before,
began to seem like a sellout.

Inevitably, the Myth of Independence drew Lynn out of
her relationship with Andy. She no longer wanted to be
reassured or even reminded of her femininity, and she began to distrust even his sexual attraction to her. "I entered a
phase," Lynn says, "where I did just about anything to be
unattractive. I stopped shaving my legs, and threw away
what little makeup I ever owned. I dressed in drab colors,
and wore sexless suits to class. Partly it was a reaction to the
gropers. I didn't want to give off any hints. I wanted to be
sure that people saw me as competent and wanted me
around for my brains, not for the way I looked. That carried over into my private life, where I didn't want to be
loved for the way I looked. Being sexy meant being a
bimbo." Like her mother, Lynn believed femininity and
competence were incompatible—unlike her mother, she
chose competence. But it was still only half an answer.

At first feminism seemed to promise an end to Lynn's life
as an outsider, giving her a way to feel both womanly and
competent, even to share something with other women. Yet
sisterhood grew out of a shared belief in women as victims.
Feminism allowed Lynn for the first time to think of herself
as a woman, but it gave her no positive way to *be* one. Even
in her work on women's history, Lynn had devoted herself

to recording the wrongs done to women and their feeble attempts at recovery. For what was women's history but the story of housewives, women who lived by the role Lynn herself despised? Like all revolutions, feminism opened more wounds than it healed. That was to be the case in Lynn's private battle.

Where Is the Middle Ground?

In 1976 Lynn Feldman won a three-year appointment to an Ivy League university's history department. She would be the first woman ever to set foot in the faculty lounges and offices as a full-fledged member. She packed her bags and left home once again for a life she pictured as ideal. But what she'd thought of as a chance to prove herself turned quickly into a struggle for survival more perilous than any that might have stemmed from marriage to Andy. While her male professors at her former university hadn't known what to make of Lynn Feldman, her colleagues now saw her as a direct threat. There was no more groping. Assistant Professor Feldman was completely off limits.

"From the start, all I felt was their resentment," Lynn says. Even dressed in her conservative tweed suit, teaching the same courses as her male colleagues, Lynn overheard a number of her fellow professors muttering, "Well, I guess they had to hire a woman." Although she'd had plenty of experience with sexism in graduate school, Lynn had somehow hoped for more respect once she'd earned her degree. Instead, says Lynn, "there I was thinking I was one of them and all they could do was see me as alien, someone who was there to meet a quota and who might one day take their job away. I lost my illusions fast about finding colleagues here. It's been particularly painful to feel that I share so much with these men—their dedication to their research, their concern for educating young minds—and then over and over again to be separated out, or even worse, simply ignored, because I'm female."

In her second and third years, Professor Feldman began offering courses in women's studies. "It was my specialty, and I believed the courses would help my women students who would someday be out there facing exactly what I'm facing now," Lynn explains. As in her graduate student days, and indeed in most of her life, Lynn's response to adversity was to go her own way, neither forcing a confrontation nor attempting a reconciliation. But without the support of her department, and with the political apathy of the late 1970s, her enrollments were slim. Accustomed to dividing her time in graduate school among her work, a group of supportive women friends, and her home life with Andy, Lynn found herself suddenly more isolated than she'd been since high school.

"I can't tell you how many hours I've spent alone in this room," Lynn tells me, "knowing that upstairs the men are talking to each other about their lives and their research. I've walked in on those conversations in the lounge. At first I just noticed this painful shifting of gears; they always changed the subject and never made any effort to include me. Now they stop talking, period." Too shy and too proud to join in with the men as Ellen Barnes would have, Lynn never learned to break those silences. "They knew how to get to me," Lynn says. "It was a freeze-out that was calculated to force me out of the running for tenure. If they kept me out of their circle, I would never be seen as a contender. All of us knew that just a few asssistant professors would be rehired—and those men knew one easy way to cut down on the competition."

Lynn's efforts in the social sphere were just as ill-fated. After several months of pleasant solitude, she reentered the dating scene, which she now realized wasn't confined to Highland Park High or Wellesley College. And still the petty rituals of showing off and being watched seemed painful and false to her. "Either there was the kind of guy who saw me only as a prospective lay, who says, 'Now kindly remove your mind with your glasses and go to bed with me.' Or there were the men who were desperately trying to get my approval, telling me how wonderful I was and putting me on a pedestal. That just makes me feel silly. They weren't really seeing me either. It always comes down to this confrontation: Will you gratify me or not? Will you sleep with me or not? Sex is the only kind of closeness men aren't afraid of—and of course sex is not really close if you don't *know* each other. Men have very little concept of women as comrades and colleagues and friends and people you can tell your *life* to. They are afraid to identify with women in a very profound way—they don't really *want* to know you. Men are still very defensive about their lives and about their feelings. They don't want to show weakness, they don't want to show *anything*—and they know women do, so you end up representing all the things they hate."

Like other feminists, Lynn had developed a female chauvinism, despising male traits every bit as much as she suspected men despised female ones. And like other women I interviewed, Lynn was left to look for a lover who would be an exception to the male rule. Her high standards put an enormous strain on first encounters, so often a matter of petty banter. As with many women whose fathers were distant breadwinners and whose mothers accepted severely limited roles within their marriages without complaint, Lynn had little notion of how a woman could break through empty social formalities to make a meaningful connection with a man. Men were as much a mystery to her as she complained women were to men. Her one close relationship with Andy, really a sexualized teacher-student relationship, had taught her nothing about reaching a man, or standing up for herself—only about how to protect herself, and how to escape.

"Most of my dates end in a kind of standoff," Lynn continues. "I feel I have to stay vigilant in my own defense—and they sense I just don't want them around anymore. It's not that I'm not interested in a relationship. I don't want my whole life to pass before I have another extended relationship. But it's hard to find a middle ground where I can get to know a man. Closeness means *so much* to me that I can't tolerate the games people play, the petty power struggles and seductions that cheapen practically every encounter."

But power is an inevitable part of any love relationship, as indeed it is present in all relationships, professional and personal. Unlike the Professional, the Feminist cannot admire any show of strength in others, nor does she wish to be admired herself. For Lynn, any power struggle implied an eventual victim, usually the woman. She fantasized an almost utopian, egalitarian closeness, ignoring the basic motivation of lovers of both sexes: to possess and be possessed. She could not let herself be wanted, nor could she want a man as she continued to doubt her ability to survive passion. Lynn was floundering in a world whose requirements for self-assertion she despised. And in it both her professional and personal goals continued to recede.

The Last Angry Woman

Ultimately Lynn's fears were confirmed. In the fall of her third year, the university notified her she would not be rehired. Assistant Professor Feldman was allowed a fourth year as a sweetener, but then she would have to go. Suffering a double disillusionment—in both professional and private life—Lynn reached a new level of rage. "I am angry about a whole lot of things that I was never angry about before," Lynn says. "I take everything very personally now. I feel very angry about the kind of education I got, that didn't prepare me for this, and about the hypocrisy in universities that hire women to satisfy quotas and then let them go. I'm angry that most of the professors here never even bothered to learn my name, or at least never address me by it. I recognize now that such things can happen to me, that I'm not the exception who can make it in the world of academics when no other woman has before. Instead I find I'm being rejected for all the things I like best about myself—and there's no way I could possibly change them."

Lynn found herself lonelier than ever, as she began to see that the path of the idealist—no matter how well-traveled—was a dead end. Feminism had proved no more certain an anchor in the world than Andy's love. Her single life no longer seemed a noble adventure, but a reminder of lost hopes.

Even though she is still angry with men, Lynn now finds herself longing to be in love with one, a combination that leaves her perpetually frustrated. Without even the satisfaction of her work to fall back on, Lynn admits she's been thinking back to her years with Andy, now a full professor who has married and started a family. "I don't know why I was so sure things couldn't continue the way they were going," she muses. "We had a comfortable life together. He was a history professor, I was a bright graduate student. He had his office at home, mine was in the library. I see now that I could have looked for a job nearby, but at the time I couldn't imagine myself being married and working. I thought I had to go off and do this job all by myself. I felt I had to choose self-reliance—or relinquish everything in order to be in a relationship. Why couldn't I see that I could do both?

"I don't regret doing what I did," Lynn continues. "But I know I have a lot to learn about softening. I don't have to tough it out all the time. I don't have to be totally self-contained and alone. Life is richer than that, a relationship is richer than that. I used to expect that if I got married, I would just freeze. But now I feel that I've come as far as I can alone. I would like to find some middle ground. I would like to know how I can stop feeling angry.

"Sometimes I don't even know how much of the anger is mine and how much I am carrying for all women. When a man makes a crude remark or treats me badly, I can never let it go. I think, I can't allow this to happen, because it could happen again, if not to me, then to some other woman. And there seem to be fewer and fewer women left who are willing to fight. I sometimes feel I'm the only one left who sees all the wrong in the world. And that means I have trouble seeing the 'just me' in a situation: what's best for *me*, what *I* feel.

"For a long time, I thought feminism explained everything. It taught me how to analyze what was going on between me and the men I lived and worked with. But now it's left me out on a limb, feeling angry with nowhere to go and no way to turn back. It's one thing to have a room of one's own—but can you live your whole life in it?"

As I left Lynn Feldman at work over her books and papers, I walked across the brick and ivy campus, watching the students, men and women, mingling, talking, arguing, laughing together. Coeducation seemed to be working out in the open air. Feminism brought these young women students here, though few, I knew from recent surveys, would call themselves feminists. Sadly, the pathfinders like Lynn Feldman who envisioned this world have not participated in it. Their fight, and the anger they carried with them on behalf of women before them, left the feminists on the defensive, unable to love, estranged, even, from their own feelings. Women like Lynn Feldman would be forever uncertain where politics ended and their own private fears and desires began.

Lynn Feldman grew up in a complex time of change—when many wrongs were being corrected, but many good things were accidentally damaged. In the new feminist world, many of the empty social games that had separated Lynn from her classmates at Wellesley were no longer in evidence. She would not be made to feel a misfit for living with a man, testing a relationship before marriage. And with living alone now simply another option, rather than a defiant social experiment, women like Lynn need no longer feel they have to "choose self-reliance—or relinquish everything in order to be in a relationship."

In the early years, the feminist campaign placed such a high value on independence that its supporters could only become isolated. Feminism overlooked the fact that coping with separation wasn't the only task of growing up. Discovering intimacy was equally important, and for a loner like Lynn probably more difficult than finding independence. In some cases, the Myth of Independence simply played on personal fears of closeness, exaggerating them beyond the point of recovery.

Feminism gave legitimacy to the panicky fear of intimacy

women like Lynn derived from their mothers' examples of self-sacrifice in marriage. Inevitably, the Feminist found it impossible to love the oppressor, to love a man whom she feared would take and never give. It is impossible to love when we are battling for selfhood, and when sex seems a part of that terrible power struggle.

But for other women, sex itself became the battlefield. That is where the Sexual Revolutionary chose to wage her private war.

3 § The Sexual Revolutionary: Rikki Sanchez

*"I developed this frame of mind about sex: if you want it,
have it. It's no big deal."*

Make Love Not War

In 1966 Robert Rimmer published *The Harrad Experiment*, a
novel about a fictional New England college run by experimental psychologists who planned to test the theories of
popular free-love advocates like Wilhelm Reich, Abraham
Maslow and Fritz Perls on a crew of willing eighteen-year-
olds. At Harrad College, male and female students shared
rooms, attended co-ed gym classes in the nude, and took
required courses in sex and contraception under the guidance of a faculty that "encouraged premarital relations
among [the] student body." The Harrad Experiment, Rimmer wrote, "would provide the blueprint for a new sexually
oriented aristocracy of individual men and women who
were free of sexual inhibitions, repression, and hate, and
were thoroughly educated into the meaning and the art of
love."

The book went through forty printings in a decade and
developed a cult following on college campuses, capturing
the imaginations of young adults eager to start a revolution
in sexual mores. In 1966 *The Harrad Experiment* seemed as
far off as 2001. While more eighteen-year-olds than ever
before were leaving home for college, and the proportion of

women among them was rising steadily, students were still governed by strict parietal rules that confined women to their rooms at night and permitted male visitors only in public parlors. For most college women, the only available means of contraception was saying no. To furtive college lovers of the mid-1960s, the notion of couples living together in the same dormitory, let alone in the same room, seemed positively utopian.

But it didn't take long to change all that. As the Vietnam War escalated and the draft tightened its grasp on eighteen-year-old men, college students began thinking of themselves as adults, and refused to submit to the rules of an earlier, repressive era. The baby boom generation flooded the campuses and new dorms had to be built; under the pressure of student demands, and often for simple convenience, most of these high-rise monstrosities became coeducational. As draft counseling centers proliferated for men, so did free clinics for women. By 1970, many college infirmaries themselves dispensed the Pill, the miracle contraceptive that was first prescribed in the United States in 1960. "Make love not war" became the battle cry of an entire generation.

In the early 1970s, the small New England college I attended seemed pretty much identical with the fictional Harrad. Sexual experimentation was part of the education, even if it was extracurricular. New couples appeared each morning at breakfast; some romances lasted long enough for couples to take up residence in each other's rooms, sometimes even assigned there by the campus housing office. Women students who once merely tallied up the number of football weekends attended each year now compared notes on how many men a semester, how many orgasms a night.

It seemed like liberation—but was it really? Years later, a college friend admitted she'd been faking orgasms with her lover and delivering false progress reports at our bull sessions. It took her ten years and a marriage to find genuine sexual satisfaction. In the late 1970s, studies by a number of university psychologists found that co-ed living often inhibited sexual desire, creating sibling attachments between the sexes instead of mature sexual ones. The women I interviewed who had attended college during the sexual revolution had other charges to make. While they claimed to be grateful to have escaped the rigid morality of the 1950s, many now admitted to finding mostly heartbreak and alienation in the moral vacuum that appeared once parietals were eliminated. "Most of my friends came to college as virgins," said one woman, "and all of us lost our virginity there, usually in our second year. But most of us ended up in very troubled, rocky, unsatisfactory relationships. There was a lot of pain. There were a lot of crushes that went unfulfilled and a lot of trying something out for one night and then feeling awful about it the next morning. There was none of the rollicking fun, joviality and freeness and nudity that was supposed to be going on. There was just a lot of shit." Many women feared their early adherence to the free sex ethic and their years of confused experimentation had set them loose in a wilderness where love and sex would never meet.

Sexual adventuring is hardly new to the single girl. Teenagers were sneaking sex in the backseats of cars or on blankets in parks long before the sexual revolution brought them into dormitory bedrooms. In the days when single women could not hitchhike across country, backpack in the wilderness, or test their independence in the many ways men could, sex was practically the unmarried woman's only adventure, her one means of rebellion. The sexual revolution didn't eliminate the old meanings of teenaged sex: the delirious searching, the rebellion, and the lonely guilt and self-doubt. It simply broadened the base and lowered the age for sexual experimentation, until by 1980 studies showed that high-school girls were far more likely to be sexually active than boys. The effect wasn't quite what Harrad's Robert Rimmer had envisioned.

The psychiatrist Herbert Hendin interviewed women students at Columbia University during the early 1970s and found that the free sex movement was doing little to make women healthier, better adjusted or more loving. "Society's increased tolerance of the sexually free woman has not yet been marked by any simultaneous increase in the young woman's confidence in her ability to handle relationships," he wrote in his 1975 book *The Age of Sensation*. "The flight from intimacy and love has been virtually institutionalized in the changes begun by the sexual revolution." The sexual revolution wasn't really freeing women after all. Instead, as one woman told me, "I felt pressured to prove I was a liberated woman and could do whatever I wanted—even though most of the time I really didn't want to be sleeping with the men I was proving myself to. I didn't learn to say no until I was thirty—*that* was truly liberating."

The sexual revolution reached the women of the Control Generation just when they were most vulnerable: in the midst of their search for sexual, professional and social identity. As much as any of the movements of the time, it yanked women away from the rules of their parents' generation and cost them the support of family and of committed love relationships at this critical juncture in their lives. One woman confided, "I was raised by very straight parents, who never talked about sex and never showed any physical affection in front of the kids. When I got to college it was like entering another world. Every woman I knew was on the Pill, and if she wasn't already sleeping with a man, she wanted to be. I started sleeping around too, because even if I didn't have my parents' approval, I knew I had society's. No one else cared."

Left with the feeling that no one cared even as she was discovering the most intimate of human connections, the Sexual Revolutionary was destined for a life of conflict about intimacy. It was to be a sad irony that women like Rikki Sanchez, who prided themselves on their openness to experience, would be tormented by an inability to trust and love.

Martyr's Daughter

While Ellen Barnes wanted to prove she was the equal of men, and Lynn Feldman tried to do without them, Rikki Sanchez played out her uncertainty about the place of women by engaging in an endless power struggle with the opposite sex. Ironically, while she feared closeness every bit as much as the Professional or the Feminist, sexual affairs occupied center stage in her life just as work and politics had taken over Ellen's and Lynn's. When we met, Rikki was, typically, in the midst of a romantic crisis that she believed would be her last. If she could decide between the two men in her life, she told me, Rikki Sanchez, Sexual Revolutionary, would settle down into monogamy and motherhood. But as we talked I began to wonder whether this crisis wasn't just one more in a series of diversions that kept Rikki from satisfying her underlying need for intimacy, and her tremendous capacity for love.

Rikki Sanchez asked me to meet her in the pale-fuchsia-and-pink lounge of the prestigious women's health club she owns and manages in downtown Houston. Rikki wasn't sure which of two lovers she'd be spending the night with so, she said, it would be easiest to meet here after her long day of supervising workouts and administering acupressure massage. At nine that night she herded her slim exercise instructors and a few plump stragglers out the spa door with the relaxed authority of a cattle rancher, and sat down on a soft gray couch to talk.

Tall, large-boned and athletic, Rikki Sanchez seemed made for life in this sprawling boomtown. At thirty-two, she was one of the most successful women I interviewed, but she had come from one of the humblest origins. She grew up in a small working-class development on the outskirts of town in the days when Houston was little more than a collection of oil derricks and ranch houses. Rikki's father, a naturalized Mexican-American who worked odd jobs as a handyman, contributed little to the family's finances, and Rikki and her three younger brothers were raised on the nurse's salary of her Texan mother. Family legend had it that Rikki's father was the best her mother, then a thirty-year-old spinster, could get.

By the time Rikki was in her twenties, Houston had grown into a town of entrepreneurs and its doors were open to a woman with energy and ambition. Chiefly, Rikki says, it was the exploitation of her mother that drove her to early achievement. "The anonymity of my mother's job really appalled me," Rikki says. "My mother performed a very valuable service, but around the hospital, she was just one of the girls. Everybody jumped for the male surgeons and specialists who were making the real bucks but never paid a bit of attention to the women who were doing all the work. My mother and the rest of the girls just stayed there year after year, never making any more money, never getting anything for all their work. I'd stop in occasionally at her ward and see the women in their little white dresses and shoes scurrying around or pushing papers in their glassed-in booths. The men would be striding through to their offices with the good views and the good furniture. She was being exploited, and she just thanked her lucky stars that she had a job. I got a lot of my willpower from her, and I knew when I grew up I would be a working woman too. But that was the extent of the similarity. She would remain in her glassed-in cubicle, and I would be heading for her boss's office."

At home, Mrs. Sanchez's example was just as bleak. Rikki's father ruled the family imperiously even though, as an angry man given to drinking binges, he was often the cause of the family's deepest financial and emotional crises. "My father is the definition of the word macho," Rikki says, "and my mother really suffered for it. One time when I was about eight years old, he and my mother had a fight and he would not give in. He made my mother leave his bedroom and sleep in the same room with my younger brothers and me for an entire year. He didn't back down until we moved to a different house.

"I can hardly remember their fighting after that," Rikki continues. "My mother is a real martyr. She can constantly eat dirt and never lose her temper. After that blowup, she worked out a system for herself out of self-defense: she started working the graveyard shift to be out of the house during the night. Then she'd come back in time to get us ready for school, and do some housework. She'd always be there working at home, fixing dinner when we got back from school—she'd have to have it on the table at a certain time for my father, or he'd raise hell. Because I was the oldest, I ended up with a lot of the responsibility for raising my three brothers, and I was supposed to be her little ally in the battle to get my father to stay peaceful. I covered up for her on the housework she didn't have time to do. I think she must have loved him, or she probably wouldn't have stayed with him all that time—but all I saw was that she took it and took it, and made us kids take it from my father as well. He was always right, and we had to make the best of it."

Like many girls forced into a parental role in a household with sexually estranged parents, Rikki's sex life began early and, not surprisingly, in a series of relationships where she too played the martyr. With her quick wits and iron willpower, Rikki had whizzed through high school trailing a string of A report cards. She was set to attend Rice University on scholarship when she met a twenty-year-old private on leave and followed him to the West Texas army base where he was stationed for his last year. "I think it was good for me," Rikki recalls. "I was so used to doing everything my parents wanted, following the straight and narrow, that I had never questioned anything before. Suddenly I felt that I didn't know why I was going to college, except maybe to please my parents who had never gone. It wasn't for *me*. I wanted to do something that was just *mine*. Running off for a passionate love affair was something my mother never would have done."

Rikki's first flight, then, was one away from her deadening homelife, a flight to feeling. But her impulsive decision soon earned her the wrath of two men. Her father refused to talk or write to her during the whole year she was away, and her young army lover made it clear he was not ready for a commitment. Working days as a waitress, Rikki spent many lonely nights in the apartment she had rented for the two of them, waiting for his weekend visits. Before long, she discovered he was spending his weekends elsewhere and Rikki's "passionate love affair" began to look like something quite different. "I was so desperate for physical affection," Rikki says now, "that I followed him to the base before I knew what was going on between us—and then I found out that nothing was. I had seen so little love and affection between my parents that I had come to equate sex with love. I thought if he was attracted to me, then we had what my parents didn't. It took me a long time to find out how wrong I was. After I left the base I got into another relationship that was even more abusive. I gave up the Rice scholarship again and moved to Austin to live with a pre-med student. At least this time I was in school; I started as a freshman at the university even though it wasn't as good a school as Rice. But I never questioned that I would go after a man rather than do what was best for myself. In fact, following a man *did* seem best for me, because I thought I was going to have a love affair that was so much better than my parents' marriage it would solve all my problems. I didn't see that I had just exchanged doing what pleased my parents for doing what pleased a man.

"My second lover, Frank, was so abusive I finally learned my lesson. I got pregnant twice, and each time he beat me up and threw me out. I had an abortion each time. This was before abortion was legal in Texas, and Frank helped me find a doctor who would do it. But after the second one, I just decided I'd had enough hurt. I moved into an apartment of my own, and really got into my schoolwork. I started to take control of my life."

Sex Addict

Once a lonely teenager who sought sex as a sign of affection, Rikki Sanchez was now determined never again to let herself be swayed by emotion. Away at college, Rikki fell in with the sexual revolution and began to enjoy sex for its own sake. If there was any emotional contact to her brief encounters, Rikki made it work to her advantage: she found that sex could be a way of manipulating others as long as she kept her own fragile emotions in check. Like many women in the era of sexual freedom, Rikki had opened up her heart and her body only to find herself dangerously exposed. It would be some time before she made herself so vulnerable again.

"I realized that even though I had rejected my mother's way of life," Rikki says of her early loves, "for a long time I tried to be like her, to be quiet and accepting when things were going wrong. I saw myself as a victim, and that bad things happened to me. But after the second abortion, and I ended that relationship, I decided that being a victim had been my choice. At college I saw women around me who knew how to get what they wanted from men. The whole ethic was that men were fun but expendable; they were like dessert. I developed this frame of mind about sex: if you want it, have it. It's no big deal.

"So I studied as hard as I could, that was my *real* life, the life I wanted to protect. And in my free time, my recreation was picking up a man at the student bar, usually some guy I'd noticed in my classes, and spending the night with him. I developed an addiction to one-night stands. I used to think—in fact, I still think this is true—that the chase was the most lovely thing about romance. You feel a delicious kind of insecurity when you aren't sure the person likes you and finally you find out he does. The buildup was always really nice, more exciting than actually being with him. And I found out I could have the physical affection I needed without the pain of breaking up if I kicked him out first thing in the morning. That felt good.

"Because aside from the chase, the wonderful thing was that I was in control. It wasn't like my other affairs where I was at some guy's mercy. I was calling the shots, and I could control the affair as long as it didn't get too serious. I always broke things off: I was very proud of the fact that I had never been dumped. Even in those two long relationships, I was the one who finally walked out. Those were the women's movement years, and I remember thinking it was strange I never felt a very strong connection with feminism, because I certainly agreed with it. But I guess I was using men more than they were using me. I was playing out my anger *with* men."

But ultimately Rikki's promiscuity ran its course. As she

graduated from college and tried to find her place in the adult world, casual sex became less satisfying. She found herself once again caught up in her family's tragedies, and once again reminded of her lack of supportive human connections. She would have to find some way of bringing love back into sex, though at first, like many women, her reaction was to run from both.

"I kept up my seduction habit all the way through college and for several years afterward when I started working for one of the small Houston oil companies," Rikki says. "That was a hard time for me, because I had whizzed through college in three years, working as a waitress part time and saving to go to business school. But then my father had an accident on the job and couldn't work at all for about a year. Since he was self-employed, he didn't have any disability insurance, so I gave my mother all my business school money. She didn't ask for it, but I couldn't feel right about keeping it when they were having trouble even paying the rent. She took it without a word of thanks. She was so used to giving and giving, she took it for granted that I would too.

"But after giving up business school, I led a very wild life. I was making all kinds of money in the oil business, but the money didn't make me happy. I was still going on sex binges. I was sleeping with fifty or sixty different men a year. I didn't even bother to count. I really was addicted to quick fixes of affection, and I wasn't in control anymore. Even though I never really got that turned on, if I didn't have sex every few days, I'd get anxious: I hated to go to bed by myself, and I hated waking up by myself. But if I brought a man home, as soon as he started talking the next morning, I wanted him out of there. And gradually I realized I didn't feel so good the day after. I used to go out again the next night and try to cheer myself up by picking up another man who might be better than the last one, and then the whole pattern would start over again."

Just as her life seemed to be spinning out of control, Rikki made a discovery that was to change everything. "I had begun to feel very distant from myself, and from my body," Rikki recalls. "I was very hyper about work because it was the one constant in my life, and I had to do a lot of wheeling and dealing to stay ahead. And I'd really lost control of my personal life. A friend suggested I take a massage series at a new health center in town, and after a while I started to enjoy going in for my massage so much that I decided to learn how to give them. I got so involved in the center that I stopped my manic sleeping around. In fact I was celibate for months. I started building up some massage clients in my spare time, and I found out it was something I enjoyed much more than the oil business. I could see the results in people, and I was building relationships that weren't just based on buying and selling."

Rikki took her oil savings and started her own health club, capitalizing on the fitness craze in her special way. "When I set up this club," Rikki says, "I planned it as a place where women could come as a kind of haven, with massage as the specialty. We provide a whole range of services here—exercise, weight training and nutrition advice. But what everyone keeps coming back for is me and my massages. It's one of the best things that ever happened to me. I am so loved at this club, I have so much support here. It's made me feel comfortable about just being myself in a way I never did before.

"There was never much touching in my family," Rikki continues, "so to have this touching during massage and to have it be nonsexual is just wonderful. I work on a very compassionate level. My whole heart gets involved. Some of the women talk to me about what's going on in their lives, and sometimes I just know they're in some kind of trouble by the way they carry themselves. When that happens, something is awakened in me and I'm right there with them. I become extremely sensitive to the points of tension in their body and to my own body as well. I love the touching. It reaches deep inside me. It's not at all like sex. There are very few people that I can even talk to on that level. Not even the two guys I've been seeing lately, Danny and Paul."

Rikki's voice turns suddenly subdued as she describes her

still problematic personal life. "I met Paul in the oil business around the time I decided to quit and start the club,"
Rikki explains. "He was working for the same company,
but he wasn't a go-getter like me. That didn't matter because Paul is emotionally one of the most phenomenal men
I have ever met. When I opened the club, for the first year
or so I was just a basket case. I would show up on Paul's
doorstep at nine-thirty at night after I had closed out the
place, after working without a break since six-thirty in the
morning. Sometimes all I could do was cry because I was so
tired. Paul never asked anything of me—nothing. He
would pick me up, take me to the bedroom, tuck me under
the covers, and turn on the television or give me a book.
After a while he'd bring me tea and crackers, and he'd give
me hugs and kisses. Then we'd go to sleep and that would
be it.

"Paul was just perfect for me then, and I still love him.
The funny thing about him is that he is a phenomenal
lover, but I don't always want to have sex with him. It
frightens me somehow. When things settled down at the
club, I met Danny. He's an entrepreneur who wanted to
help me franchise the club—which I don't want to do. At
least not yet. But Danny is tremendously sexy. We have
great times in bed, but we don't talk much the way I do
with Paul. Sometimes I tell myself there's nothing wrong
with having two lovers. They don't know about each other,
so nobody is getting hurt. Maybe I need to have several
different lovers to satisfy the different sides of my nature,
to be complete. But lately I've been thinking I'm going to
have to choose. I'm thirty-two now and I'd like to have
children. A lot of women my age are having their first kids,
and I just envy them so much. I feel like I'm ready for the
responsibility—I certainly have the money, and now that
the club is under control, I have the time. But how can I do
that with two men in my life?"

Sex and the Self

Although Rikki Sanchez's story is one of extremes, the basic patterns are common. The Sexual Revolutionary believed that she had achieved the sexual freedom and openness to experience that once men alone were allowed. In Rikki's case, what she called her "sex binges" actually imitated her father's alcoholic binges that had dominated the emotional life of the family. Yet inwardly, as Rikki and others confided, promiscuity wasn't satisfying, either sexually or emotionally. Instead, it served a quite opposite purpose: "free" sex was a way of warding off intense feeling, either good or bad, protecting a woman from the ultimate disappointment of loving she had witnessed in so many older women. "The sexual revolution gave me a good crutch," one woman admitted. "Promiscuity keeps men at a distance. When I get hurt by one man, my reaction is to go out with every man I can and sleep with most of them— and then the next day I think, My God, what have I done? Then, if I'm starting to really like one guy, I will go find four others and sleep with them to see if any of them will divert my attention."

This syndrome was especially common among successful women who seemed to believe that brief, unsatisfactory love affairs were the dues they paid for success. Women like Rikki still lived by the fear-of-success ethic they inherited from mothers who believed no woman could succeed at both love and work. They had rebelled against traditional femininity by choosing work, but few women of the Control Generation could achieve both professional and personal fulfillment without feeling guilty. While they might allow themselves satisfaction in work, they denied themselves contentment in love, for success in both would be too threatening to their needy and dependent mothers. Rikki actually tried to forfeit both forms of success to her mother: handing over her business school money and maintaining a self-destructive cycle of sexual flings followed by depression. The combination was alarmingly similar to her mother's own acceptance of suffering in both love and work.

Rikki was too much a survivor to stay down for long, yet it was difficult for women like Rikki to see where they'd gone wrong. Rikki believed self-control and aggression were the elements missing from her mother's life. At least *she* was doing the rejecting, Rikki reassured herself after her binges. Manipulation was a skill she possessed that her martyred mother did not. Yet it was a power that never got her very far, as long as she used it to ward off intimacy. Deep down, she continued to believe that love itself would be her undoing, as it had been her mother's.

While the sexual revolution aggravated the ambivalence about femininity that had been passed from mother to daughter for generations, it also raised new questions about sex itself. Like other movements affecting women's lives in the late 1960s and 1970s, the sexual revolution promoted male standards over traditional female ones. In 1966, the same year *The Harrad Experiment* appeared, Masters and Johnson published data showing that the female orgasm, long considered by psychiatrists to be mysteriously elusive, actually resembled the predictable patterns of arousal in men. The multiple orgasm made headlines, and women, encouraged by a sex-conscious press, set out on a quest for sexual pleasure like so many female Don Juans. If nothing else, casual sex could save them from the deadening bonds of marriage that so constricted their mothers.

The cult of the orgasm became part of the Myth of Independence, encouraging sex as a purely physical, even solitary act. Even with a partner, women were counseled in countless magazine advice columns and sex manuals to attend primarily to their own satisfaction. Nonorgasmic women were told to work up to orgasm in intercourse by first practicing masturbation alone. The new emphasis on sexual mechanics ignored the emotional sources of sexual pleasure, and implied that women did not need a committed relationship, or even a man, to enjoy themselves in bed. While most studies showed that women usually did not reach their sexual peak until their late twenties, no one connected this with the fact that those were most likely the years of their peak emotional experiences as well.

While the research on orgasms helped women to think of themselves as sexual beings, rather than as the solely reproductive agents they'd been in the feminine mystique years, it overlooked real differences between male and female sexuality that came out in later studies as women experimented with sex more freely. By the mid-1970s, new research showed that women needed more time for arousal than men, rarely enjoyed sex outside an emotional context, and tended to feel guilty about one-night stands and even about masturbation. Just as women were setting out to liberate their sexuality, they were caught in a fog of myths and contrary data. Affectionate sex was something women had to rediscover. "It took me a long time to find out there's nothing satisfying about getting laid," one woman told me. "You just end up feeling empty and silly about it."

More seriously, some experts contended that early and random sexual experimentation could be damaging to a woman's developing psyche. "I see terrible damage resulting from being penetrated too young," claims Dr. Judianne Densen-Gerber of the Menninger Clinic, who places the minimum age for first sexual intercourse at eighteen. "It seems that one can't bear the invasion of one's inner territory until one is truly ready for an adult love relationship." Rikki Sanchez's account of her sexual development seemed to bear this out. "All that time, wild as I was," Rikki recalls, "I never felt that involved in sex. I always felt separate from what I was doing, like I was another person outside my body, watching what was going on from some point on the ceiling. I felt OK while we were taking our clothes off and getting to know each other's bodies—that was still part of the game. But then some part of me would shut down. I could enjoy myself, I got a charge out of it—but it was nothing like what I later felt sometimes with Paul. Then I felt safe, and loved, and I could feel whatever I wanted—that was *really* scary."

Rikki gave her body up to invasion, but in an unconscious form of self-protection, she learned to hold her self apart. By the time she wanted intimacy, this separation of self and body, spirit and flesh, kept her from realizing all that was possible in this most intimate act. She could not entrust herself to a man.

Danny or Paul: Another False Choice

But Rikki claimed the unhealthy pattern was ending. All she had to do was choose between Danny and Paul, settle down with her selection, and her days of sexual addiction would be over. I had heard of the same dilemma from other women, several of whom seemed to enjoy it. One thirty-four-year-old engineer told me, "Out in public, I like men who are very powerful and influential in their fields, but privately I like very sensitive men—and the two qualities almost never come together. Some of the happiest, most even times in my life were when I was dating two people: one was sensitive, and the other was the live wire." Yet such women were often hard drivers who could not reconcile their own inner conflict between power and sensitivity. Double affairs provided "even times" in these women's lives because they maintained an important internal split.

Rikki's choice was not between power and sensitivity but between two kinds of loving, neither of which was very deep. As she described the two men, it seemed impossible to choose between them. The silent, undemanding, tremendously sexy Danny was a reminder of Rikki's sex addict past. Paul, the man whose hugs she preferred to his lovemaking, provided the unwavering affection that Rikki had never received from her embattled parents. As long as Rikki could turn to Danny for sex, she would not have to face the challenge of mutually involving love that she had glimpsed in her few "scary" love scenes with Paul. For a woman to whom love meant either overpowering someone, or being overpowered, the arrangement was ideal.

Sometimes the choices we present ourselves can never be satisfactorily made, only interpreted. How could Rikki believe she was ready to settle down and raise children when she was unable to choose between two potential husbands, neither of whom offered a sound basis for starting a family? Just as Ellen Barnes's inability to decide between a law partnership and a lover showed her deep ambivalence about forming permanent attachments, so did Rikki's choice betray a fear that to accept affection, once the staple of the adult woman's world, would ruin her. As long as she juggled Danny and Paul, her life as a mother-figure would be held in abeyance. For these women, loving was still an all-or-nothing proposition, one they deliberately avoided by setting themselves conflicting objects of loyalty. Unable to choose, they thwarted love in the belief that they were saving themselves.

Rikki chose instead a controlled form of caring with her massages. Here she administered to women in trouble, but, unlike her mother the nurse, extracted a high wage in return. In a sense, Rikki was nurse, doctor and administrator. By relegating care to her professional life, she showed just how much it frightened her personally. In Rikki's view, her mother "got nothing" for all the care she gave as nurse, wife and mother. Rikki couldn't see the joys of caring for its own sake: she needed the financial independence it brought in a profession, and such an inducement was, of course, unavailable in family life. As a mother, she'd never be so free.

The idea of motherhood before or without marriage, as we shall see, is popular in the Control Generation, growing out of the underlying belief that taking care of children is easier than linking up with another adult. Part of not wanting to love is not trusting those who love you. As one woman said, "I can't make choices about intimacy because that would mean depending on someone. I don't let anyone help me." At this stage, independence, far from promoting psychological growth, was actually holding women back.

Predictably, the Sexual Revolutionary was the daughter of a woman whose life was also based purely on her sexual function: but in her case it was the sexuality of reproduction. Rikki's martyred mother had given her life to husband and children. For the Sexual Revolutionary, birth control had separated sex from reproduction: women no longer were at the mercy of their reproductive cycles. Yet many, like Rikki, still made sex the center of their lives; and theirs was a dangerous sexuality. The new sex took its practitioners into a world where actions were without consequences, where there was no need to develop responsibility, where women learned to abandon the care on which lasting love thrives.

The sexual revolution didn't require its proponents to grow up as they did, controlling their emotions as they regulated their pregnancies. But after witnessing the burden of commitment in their mothers, a different lover every week seemed like freedom. Sadly, that kind of freedom taught women like Rikki no more about the give-and-take of a healthy love relationship than they had learned from mothers who gave themselves totally to husbands and children. When sexual intimacy was so widely available, emotional intimacy had to be protected and often was lost: many women withheld their feelings even as they gave men their bodies.

This was to be the irony of the new movement for self-discovery: the more freedom, the harder it was to find one's bearings and the greater the tendency to set artificial boundaries on one's life. So, women defined themselves by work, by politics, by sexuality. Even the most determined Self-Seeker got lost if she believed she had to find herself by herself. For she never discovered the true self that emerges in love.

PART III
Self-Seekers

Women think too much about men. . . . They give men the power to determine their identities, their value, to accept or reject them. They have no selves. . . . Why don't they just forget about the men and be themselves?

—*Marilyn French,* The Women's Room, *1977*

In the fall of 1976, I was back in school attending a lecture in developmental psychology with over a hundred other students, most of them women and many of them seniors. Most of us, I suspected, had signed up for the course for the same reason: to ease a growing anxiety about our coming graduation when we'd be forced to make something of ourselves. But so far we'd listened only to weeks of lectures about the importance of the mother-infant bond in raising healthy male children. Today, finally, we would hear one lecture about the psychological development of women. We were just naive enough to expect some guidance.

Our widely respected male professor began his talk that day by telling us that women grow up differently from men. Girls had a puzzling tendency to prolong attachments to their mothers, he said, even as those relationships became strained in adolescence. We heard about the case of Cindy, a chronically depressed sixteen-year-old with no interest in her schoolwork, in boys or in her future, who felt happy only when she left her mother for a brief summer vacation with a friend. Our professor explained that Cindy's depression was merely an extreme version of the feelings every woman experiences as she grows up. Cindy wouldn't feel better until she found her adult identity by becoming a mother herself, starting the whole miserable process over again.

Suddenly anxious, I thought of my mother, off on another coast. I thought of my own uncertain future: I was twenty-two, the age by which, in my mother's generation, most women had married and started a family. But I had no plans for marriage and certainly none for motherhood. None of the women I knew did. Was this professor telling a lecture hall full of college-educated women we would be tormented like the teenaged Cindy until we resigned ourselves to the occupation of housewife? I had hopes of launching a career, but like Cindy, I imagined, I didn't have any clear ideas about how to do that. Could Cindy's lack of preparation for the world beyond her home be the real reason for her depression? Wouldn't the specter of a life devoted to children depress anyone on the brink of adulthood?

There was a disappointed silence in the hall. We had looked forward to this session, all of us hoping for some answers. But in the pursuit of our adult identities, it seemed we were going to have to be self-taught.

For much of history, women have found their identities by my professor's scheme: in marriage, by loving a man and mothering his children. Now that women have the freedom to choose when, and even whether, to bear children, we are free to define ourselves by what we do as much as by whom we love. Yet the opportunity to contribute more to the world than another generation of children can be as much a burden as a gift. The rites of passage that once marked woman's entrance into adulthood—engagement parties, bridal showers and weddings—have lost their meaning, with few substitutes except, perhaps, college graduation. "My friends and I floundered through our twenties waiting for the curtain to go up on our lives," one thirty-two-year-old woman told me. "We realized too late that we were already at center stage."

As I listened to more and more women across the country describe their third decade as a time of searching and confusion, I began to realize that women were going through an identity crisis: a different one from the sort my professor described, one women had never experienced before. It was no longer certain what kind of person an adult woman should be. Try as they would to reach a certain conclusion, the women of the Control Generation were struggling to find themselves, often well into their thirties.

Unlike Brave New Women, the women I call Self-Seekers found no solutions in ideology. Instead, the elements that influence all young adults as they come to know themselves—the lessons of parental models, the myths of their culture and the example of peers—seemed to overwhelm them. Most women had little sense of an inner self to anchor them. Many were raised in families in which little was expected of daughters, and they were left to acquire in adulthood the self-assurance their brothers learned as children. Others, responding to their mothers' feelings of failure, attempted to live out their mothers' lost dreams, and in the process became sadly estranged from their own innermost desires.

Sometimes I wonder what happened to those other women in my psychology class, who so dutifully scribbled notes about a kind of woman none of us wanted to become. Instinctively we knew that the narrow course of marriage and motherhood was too limited, perhaps even dangerous. But beyond that, the Myth of Independence was all we had to go on, and that code of lonely self-sufficiency was as useless an answer to our problems as Cindy's brief summer vacation was for her depression. What were we to make of the unstable love affairs most of us had tired of by our mid-twenties? And what of our periodic longings to find one man and raise a family? The only shared philosophy of our generation rejected gender as a clue to self-knowledge and wrote off love as a means of self-fulfillment. Yet was it possible to forget about the men and be ourselves?

The Self-Seeker is a product of an idealistic generation that hoped to make a complete break with the conformity

and selflessness of the traditional American woman's role.
Yet unwittingly she had set herself an impossible task. As
we shall see, the Loner, the Heroine and the Conformist all
struggle with different aspects of the Crisis in Female Identity, but all three share the unfortunate belief that solitary
self-discovery should be a woman's primary goal in life.
Inevitably, their continual striving for autonomy turned to
defensiveness and chronic fears of intimacy. Looking for
independence, they found, most often, isolation.

4 § The Loner: April Benson

"I feel most myself when I'm not in a relationship. It can be lonely, but at least my time is my own."

Family Happiness

After weeks of traveling from one urban singles complex to another, I arrived in the small southern Vermont town where April Benson lives and decided to park my car and walk the half mile out to her sculpture studio. The rolling green hills and tiny freshly painted farmhouses were a relief after so much brick and concrete, and on a far hill I witnessed a scene, rare, I imagined, even in this New England village: a mother and father, two children and a dog frolicked in the late afternoon sunlight. As I drew closer, I could see they were all holding hands.

But closer still, the group appeared a little too symmetrical, a little too balanced. This family wasn't frolicking: all five figures were caught in a rigid pose. Then I knew I had reached the sculpture garden in back of April Benson's studio. Later, when April took me to see the larger-than-life-sized piece, *Nuclear Family*, I discovered that the happy group was actually a distorted conglomeration of welded metal "found" objects: the mother's head an antique hat-maker's frame—rusty, hollow and too small for the skeletal dressmaker's dummy that supported it; the father's, a hub-cap from a junk car soldered to other used-car parts that made up the rest of his stark figure. Up close, I saw the sculpture was no blissful family tableau. Like most of April Benson's best work, now enjoying a vogue in small galleries on the West Coast and in Manhattan, it made a mockery of the institution of the family.

April herself, I saw right away, presented many of the same contradictions as her sculpture. Standing in the middle of the green hillside, dressed in overalls, with her blond hair in one long braid and her hands stained and fingernails stubby, April Benson could easily be mistaken for one of her many female neighbors: young women who moved to the country with their husbands to raise children in a clean environment, wearing out their fingers gardening, kneading bread and refinishing secondhand furniture. Even April's rented farmhouse, with its well-stocked kitchen and rooms decorated with hand-sewn curtains and well-tended houseplants, suggested family living. But while April spends many of her waking hours sculpting works of art from her ideas about families, she is a woman who openly dreads the roles of wife and mother. "I'm afraid that if I change my circumstances in any drastic way, I won't be able to work," thirty-two-year-old April told me. "I know I can be an artist living alone and supporting myself with part-time work. But you bring in other things like marriage or children . . . I'm even afraid of having a regular lover.

"In my sculpture," April continued, "I like to undermine the sweetness and sacredness of families, which are rarely as good for people as we're supposed to believe." And although April would never characterize her own family as one with unusual problems, it is there that she finds her inspiration for bitter social commentary. Expand the number of children in *Nuclear Family* to three, add two cats, and the sculpture could be the Benson family when April was growing up in White Plains, New York. It is no coincidence that the father is made of automobile parts: April's father ran a successful car dealership. And as for April's mother, "She was a full-time mother. She even had help around the house so she could put all of her professional and organizational ability into directing her children and guiding them and pushing them. She had three kids in three years and she wanted to do everything she could for us. She was totally into taking us to lessons, seeing the dentist regularly, supervising our homework."

The mother's role has preoccupied April in her most recent work, she admits, because she fears it. Peaceful as family life was for April, her mother's example offered no guidance to a woman who would come of age in the era of independence. "The series of pieces I'm working on now is based on a dream I had recently," April explains as she leads me into the big, dusty barn where she keeps her works in progress. "It was very brief, but very powerful, and it's haunted me ever since. I dreamed I was in the hospital on the operating table, and the male surgeon leaned over me and said, 'You have a choice: either we can operate on your brain or on your reproductive tract.' I woke up in a cold sweat. I was panicked!"

The anxiety flares in April's eyes as she speaks, but quickly fades as she comes upon another welded metal construction in the middle of her workroom, that looks at first like a scaled-down Statue of Liberty. "The piece I just finished," April says, "is about a woman who makes the choice. The woman is standing, and her dress is unbuttoned from the waist down. Wedged between her legs is a baby. Under one arm, against her side, is tucked a tiny little man and a tiny house. Her head is missing—sheared right off her shoulders. She's holding it up with her other arm. She lost her head, you see.

"That's my anxiety, my fear, my own personal dilemma coming out in my work," April goes on. "That woman has made the choice I could never bring myself to make. I don't want to give up my brainpower for another person. I know it sounds cold, but I have enough trouble making a living as an artist. I don't have room in my life for anyone else. That woman chose the baby, and she lost her head. She has the man under her arm. She has the house and the baby, but she lost her head."

From the Mom Generation to the Me Generation

All branches of psychology agree on the profound influence of parents on their children. In the best of circumstances, we learn from our parents the roles we will play in society. For generations, daughters grew up to be full-time mothers, satisfied with performing a task that, if not publicly influential, still guaranteed women domestic power and respect. But in the 1950s, at a time when the American family was most glorified, the chain was broken. Economic, technological and medical advances combined to permit women to play a greater part in the running of their country. They would have to fight for the chance, but suddenly women were divided into those who would fight and those who wouldn't. Rebellious daughters carried into a new world models of adult womanhood they wanted to destroy yet that dominated them all the same because they had no others. "I was angry at my mother for the way she raised me," said one woman, voicing a common complaint. "She taught me to be just like her, but when *she* grew up there was a world ready to accommodate a generation of housewives. The world changed for us—we got there and everything our mothers taught us was out of date."

Intended to raise another generation of working fathers and stay-at-home mothers, the nuclear family of the 1950s has had almost the opposite effect on its children. During the 1970s, when April Benson's generation reached their twenties, the number of American households headed by married couples dropped from 70 to 60 percent, and the number of households made up of married couples with two or more children fell to less than one in five. At the same time, the ratio of adults living alone increased until, some experts predict, by 1985 one in every four households will be occupied by just one person. And the next generation shows every sign of continuing the trend. While most teenagers still plan to marry, a multigenerational study by a pair of prominent University of Michigan researchers found that the majority believe a single life would be just as satisfying.

A nation of loners may be the inevitable product of a country founded by separatists and settled by pioneers. Yet most experts find the trend toward singleness a frightening proof of the breakdown of society itself. In his book, *An Immodest Agenda: Rebuilding America Before the 21st Century*, the sociologist Amitai Etzioni blames the fragmentation of the family on an "ego-centered mentality" which has overtaken the majority of Americans. As a result of permissive childrearing and educational practices, he argues, recent generations have come to undervalue marital and parenting commitments in favor of blind loyalty to the self. Along with writers as diverse as Christopher Lasch and Tom Wolfe, Etzioni claims America suffers from an epidemic of narcissism and predicts the disappearance of the family altogether by the next century unless a major change in attitude takes place.

Yet these alarmists fail to understand the significance of an "ego-centered mentality" for the young women who make up one of the largest groups of the new singles. Women like April Benson, often the first in their families to live alone, choose singleness not because they lack responsibility or possess an inflated sense of self-worth, but for entirely opposite reasons. Most have been so well trained in self-abnegation and in devotion to others that living alone is for them the only way to discover their innermost selves.

For women, the trend toward singleness reflects not so much a new narcissism as a vast shift in identity formation. When the sex that has held the primary responsibility for taking care of others temporarily rejects the role, critics may call it selfish. Yet the many women who now delay marriage in favor of pursuing personal interests are doing no more than men have in the past: securing their place in the world before committing themselves to relationships. Psychologists still argue that women, more than men, derive their sense of self from their connections to family, friends and lovers. But in recent years psychologist Carol Gilligan has uncovered a phase in woman's growth apparently as women themselves discovered it: the development of a relationship with the self. The traditional Mom who devoted herself to husband and children, Gilligan explains, never learned to count herself in when making choices that would affect all members of the family. Such women made "serve me last" into a way of life. The women of the Control Generation witnessed their mothers' deliberate surrender and, as they grew older, shared increasingly in their mothers' second-class status within the family. One thirty-year-old woman complained to me that her older brother still expected her to cook his breakfast when the two were home visiting their parents.

The daughters of the Mom generation never learned from their mothers what their brothers learned every day from working fathers: the ability to distance themselves from the demands of others, and the confidence to take as well as to give. They learned instead how terribly consuming relationships, based on love or on family ties, could be for women. En masse, these daughters turned against love and family relationships, cultivating instead what Gilligan calls the relationship to the self. Yet, seeing their lives in opposition to their mothers' rather than as carrying on a developmental process their mothers had only partly completed, many women were destined to become perpetual loners. Like April Benson, they lived their lives in the shadow of their childhood families even as they believed they had broken away.

One of the Girls

The Bensons of White Plains, New York, thrived on the 1950s belief in family togetherness. Unlike the mothers of Rikki Sanchez, Lynn Feldman, or Ellen Barnes, Mrs. Benson enjoyed the work of motherhood and showed no signs of regretting her total devotion to the family. Also a dedicated parent, April's father spent all his free time with the family, taking the entire crew on long summer vacations in the family station wagon. Yet the emphasis on family unity proved troubling to April Benson. Growing up protected from crime and dirt and noise could have been a privilege. But from an early age April sensed, beneath the peaceful surface of suburban life, a hidden violence to women. Little girls and mothers all were robbed of individuality in exchange for conformist femininity. Terrifying as it was, April's nightmare of the operating room choice between brains and motherhood had its source in what, during the 1950s, was a perfectly normal girlhood.

April was the middle of three children, with an older brother and a younger sister. But, says April, "my mother treated my sister and me as if we were twins. We dressed alike and shared the same room and got the same gifts for our birthdays. We were always called 'the girls,' while my brother had a name, Eric. It wasn't so much that he was the favorite. But he was a boy, and he had a future. In the end, even though my mother drove my sister and me around to just as many lessons as Eric and hounded us about our homework just as much, it was always assumed that Eric would amount to something, and we were just 'the girls.' We would grow up and get married and that would be that."

April was being educated into subservience, learning to accept second best as a fact of femininity. The April who was groomed and schooled would make a good wife in the tradition her mother thrived on. But April was to grow up into a world where passivity and lack of ambition in women were no longer survival skills. In fact, they were self-destructive. Already in childhood, the terrible choice between femininity and selfhood, body and brains, haunted her. "It was always presented to me," April recalls, "that there would be two options when I grew up: either I could be an old maid schoolteacher, or I could be like my mother. I sometimes felt afraid, because neither one seemed right. But I know I always assumed that to be like my mother was the best choice. We were always trained to think what a wonderful woman she was and what a great life she made for my father and us. Why should I want anything different?" Her training in acquiescence made it difficult even to ask such a question.

For April, as for most girls of her generation, the lessons of womanhood she saw around her offered few alternatives.

She felt, instinctively, that to be one of "the girls" was to be virtually anonymous. To grow up and become a mother would be little better since, as in her own family, motherhood meant attending exclusively to children, still with no unique identity. Worse was the choice of "old maid schoolteacher." The woman who chose brains over femininity would be denied a family; and in April's world family was everything. Combining work and motherhood was not even to be considered. "None of my friends' mothers worked," April recalls, "except for the woman next door who *had* to work. Her daughter ate lunch at my house every day, and we all felt sorry for her. In all those years I never heard what kind of work her mother did. We just knew she had to do it and that was embarrassing."

Yet in the midst of lessons and homework and birthday parties, April found something that was her own, an interest that had nothing to do with moms or old maids. At an early age, April discovered artwork as a means of setting herself apart from the staid suburban neighborhood. "I was always doing art," April recalls. "Other kids would go off and read, but I went off to draw. I became a loner, and retreated from the family. When I was young, what interested me most were scenes of real natural beauty and wildness: anything that was more alive than White Plains, New York. If my family went on camping trips, there I'd be with my sketch pad, a little way off.

"Art was my adventure and my comfort," April explains. "It was always the most alive time for me when I was drawing. I guess you could say it was a relationship—a relationship where I *was* somebody." Strangely, art was the one field in which April was not given lessons, an omission that increased her sense of private freedom when she retreated with her sketch pad. Yet while her parents approved of her sketching habit, they certainly didn't take her work seriously. "I was just cute little April with her book of scribbles," April says.

It would take April herself a good many years to think of art as her calling. Her drawing and the later cardboard-and-scrap constructions she stored in her closet were too personal, private expressions she never thought to share with family or friends, or even considered showing in public. As a girl encouraged to see herself only as a potential wife, April lacked the self-confidence to put her work forward. Then, when it came time to leave her family, April had not only the anonymity of "the girls" to fight, but the larger lessons of womanhood to overcome. April had never known a woman whose adult identity did not revolve around her marriage. And while women like Rikki and Lynn and Ellen had the examples of unhappy mothers to warn them of the dangers of subservience in love, April would have to learn from her own mistakes.

Love Stories

The Benson girls were raised on the fairy tale of their parents' romance. Like many of the women I interviewed, April could tell me in precise detail the story of how her parents fell in love. They met at a party, and for April's father it was love at first sight. But when he called to set up a date the next day, April's mother put him off. Only when April's grandmother interceded with "Give him a chance —you don't have to marry him" did the two arrange a date. But on that night, as April's mother told her daughters time and again, "I knew right then he was the man for me."

"It was like something out of a romance novel," says April. "That's the way I thought it was going to happen to me—you meet the man, you go out on a date and say, 'This is the man for me.' From then on it's smooth sailing. I went to college believing that. I'd go on a date and think, Is he the man?"

But April's first encounters with men were far from smooth sailing. Determined to leave White Plains far behind, April moved three thousand miles away in 1968, the year she turned eighteen, to attend college in California. She chose a women's college, Mills, where she could study art. But she wasn't thinking of a career. Instead, she recalls, "my friends and I were all kind of green, we hadn't dated much in high school. We were all very sensitive and we all wanted desperately to be in love. We would have severe crushes on men we met at mixers and pine and pine and pine, and it would never work out.

"My friends used to kid me," April continues, "because I told them what I liked in men was corduroy jackets and wire-rim glasses. I guess that meant brooding, intellectual types. I didn't know much about men, and neither did most of my friends. The only men I knew well were my brother and my father, both of whom were just very plain, nice guys—not the sort of men you tend to have wild crushes on in college. My mother used to say to my sister and me, 'I hope you meet someone like your father, someone as wonderful as your father.' Well, I met some nice boys, but I was never attracted to them.

"Like all the women I knew, in the end I fell for the wrong kind of man. My junior year I got involved with one of my teachers, an art historian, which was devastatingly traumatic for me. He was a real romantic figure—tall and bearded and known for having affairs with students. He made it clear from the start that he really wasn't interested in *me*. He just wanted to fuck. But he's the guy I lost my virginity with! And since this was my first physical attraction, my first powerful sexual experience, I was hooked. He was on my mind from the moment I met him for about three years straight. When I graduated from college I stayed around the Bay Area for several years just so I could be there in case he changed his mind about me. It was a real obsession, and I kept going back to him no matter how often he told me he wasn't interested in a relationship. I felt a compulsion to enter his field, to try to win him over by proving myself to him intellectually, even though I'd never thought of being an art historian. But I was never smart enough for him. He once told me he could never love me because I could only speak one language."

April shied away from the nice men like her father who might have made her a housewife. Yet she followed her mother's example closely enough to fall in love with a man and lose herself to him. She tried desperately to make herself into the woman her professor would love: a woman who didn't care about commitment even as she met his sexual needs, who would take up his subject, his city, his way of life. She had chosen a man who would prove to her what she already believed: the impossibility of staying herself in a relationship. Yet she had also chosen a man who refused to keep her around long enough for the loss to be total.

And April was gaining strengths of her own. "When I graduated and started working at a framing store in San Francisco," April says, "I began to feel a little more independent. I had my own room in an apartment I shared with all my best friends from college, and I began to feel like a real pioneer. I wasn't a mother yet, but I wasn't an old maid either. I could have all the men I wanted. I began reacting against my obsession with my teacher by being very aggressive with men. I went to parties alone, I went to bars alone—and that's when my pattern of picking men with problems started. All the men I've dated seriously since college have been very cold, and many of them have been alcoholics. I went out with a well-known painter who was much older and drank too much. Another man was a back-to-nature type, a loner. I would always be turning down some perfectly nice man in favor of cold loners and alcoholics."

April's mother continued to pressure her to marry. "Everybody my mother knows had a son or a nephew in San Francisco," April laughs, "and she'd always be trying to get me to go out with these 'nice' med students or lawyers. I used to have this fantasy that if everybody she wanted me to meet called me up, it would be like *The Night of the Living Dead*. They would all come into the apartment at the same time and say, 'Your mother sent me.' I know she wanted the best for me, but marriage just didn't fit my life back then. I was starting to take myself seriously as an artist; I even cut back my hours in the framing shop so I would have more time for myself.

"I still don't want that much of an involvement," April continues. "Sometimes when I meet men who are really nice, I feel so claustrophobic. They remind me of my brother and my father, and I start to feel my family closing in on me. So instead I pick men with problems. They give me the distance I want because I always know I could never marry them."

In 1975, April finally left San Francisco and her art-historian lover behind for Vermont. She made the move so many other women of the Control Generation chose in their mid-twenties: she left a man in order to find herself. It was just the opposite of the way her mother discovered her adult identity, but just as fruitful. Her total devotion to her work and her new belief in herself began to show in her sculpture. April Benson's work appeared in several avant-garde Manhattan galleries, and soon she had offers from the same dealers whose work she had once framed in San Francisco. She gloated that one day her old lover might walk into a waterfront gallery and see an April Benson mocking him with her own success. April Benson didn't have it all, but she had herself. And for a time that seemed like enough.

A Love Affair with the Self

From an early age, April Benson felt most alive and most secure when she was alone with her sketch pad. An activity she chose independently and that allowed her some distinction in a close-knit family, April's art soon meant more to her than a potential career. Sculpture wasn't simply an occupation in which April discovered competence her mother lacked, as the law was for Ellen Barnes. While Ellen used the discipline of the law to confine her emotions, art was full of feeling for April. During her hours in the studio she felt free to release emotions, even to explore the nature of love and families, and her personal experience with them. In April's own words, art was a relationship—"a relationship where I *was* somebody."

But what was this relationship? Whom did it really involve? In childhood, art made up, in part, for April's disappointing relationship with her intrusive yet self-denying mother, a woman who stifled her daughter's selfhood even as she gave up her own to childrearing. Art began to stand for the vulnerable self that all others ignored and that April must therefore protect. Soon she was expressing in her art the anger and confusion that she could express to no one else. The battle for self took April away from her family to study art, and was repeated again in her first and only serious love affair. From then on, her relationship to herself, embodied in her sculpture, would be an exclusive one. Lovers stayed on the sidelines, occasionally becoming the least important member of a threesome.

"I feel most myself when I'm not in a relationship," says April. "It can be lonely, but at least my time is my own. When I do have a boyfriend, I notice when dinnertime comes I start getting nervous. You have to make a million decisions and a million compromises. You have to figure out your budgets, and who's going to cook, and who's going to wash dishes. Are you going to eat cheese, are you going to make a vegetarian meal? Are you going to cook at his house or your house? And I hate spending much time in other people's houses. It really disrupts my routine. If I stay overnight, the whole morning is shot. I feel safest and most comfortable in my own house. I'm really very frightened by the idea of full-time living with someone."

And habits that began as self-protection soon grew to an instinctive fear of intimacy. "I prefer men who are not interested in long-term relationships," April continues. "When I feel a man getting too close to me, I just don't like it. When a man starts talking about marriage, or wanting to have a family, it totally turns me off. It's the kiss of death. I feel so claustrophobic. I think, Get away! Get away! I like men. But I like a lot of empty space around me. I like a lot of blocks of time without commitments. I even have recurring nightmares about having a roommate!" For April, the safest relationships were those she could control: her connection with her innermost self as expressed in her sculpture, or her more recent affairs with men in which her emotions were scarcely touched.

Women like April, who were struggling to develop inner strength, sensed they are so vulnerable to love they must set strict limits on their feelings for men. April chose a series of lovers who meant so little to her she didn't bother to name them. Seeing these men as types—one heartless alcoholic after another—was a way of preventing involvement. Ironically, she dared not recognize the individuality of her lovers even as she insisted on her own right to be respected as an individual. April's affairs allowed her to say, "I must be here because you can't get me," a formulation just the opposite of what had been her mother's recipe for self-affirmation: "I'm here because I love you."

But then, April's romantic life was based on opposition to her mother—or at least to her mother's example. The woman who repeatedly chooses dangerous or unsuitable men as lovers is almost a cliché in psychiatric literature. In his recent book, *Fathers and Daughters*, the psychiatrist William Appleton cites the accepted explanation that such women grew up repressing incestuous desires for their fathers; unreliable men seemed attractive since they did not remind these women of their much-loved fathers and the taboo they dared not break. But for women of April's generation, there is a much simpler explanation. Nice men reminded April of her father, and then of "my family closing in on me." To April, the family was a set of fixed relationships which prevented individual members from realizing their full potential. She believed that a woman who wished to find herself must do so alone, free from the burdens of the close love relationships that April had never known a woman to control. April Benson simply feared the men who would make her into a mother.

Still, while refusing at every opportunity to take on the role her mother played, April accepted the basic lessons of her mother's example: woman's capacity to merge identity with occupation, and her vulnerability to relationships. It was a mixed message that, for a woman determined to make her way outside the home, meant choosing between womanhood and selfhood, connections to others and connection to the self—and, as it came to April in her nightmare, between creativity and procreation.

The Genderless Self

As long as April Benson believed she must fight off traditional femininity to save herself, she would be tormented by decision dreams at night, and increasing indecision during many of her waking hours. For try as she would to confine her thoughts on the family to her sculpture, as she entered her mid-thirties and more of her college friends married and began to raise children, April started to worry that she'd be "the last single woman left on earth." She had no plans for motherhood, and no lover she would choose for a husband, but "I feel differently about motherhood every day," April admitted anxiously near the end of the interview. "I'm getting older and I worry that soon I won't have any choice. It disturbs me more now that the men I'm involved with are so distant. I even bring it up with them sometimes, but usually it gets me nowhere and things stay the same, or we break up. It doesn't seem to bother me enough to change the pattern. I still find myself running the other way whenever I meet an eligible man."

Like many women who believed marriage and motherhood had made their mothers little more than appendages to husband and children, April Benson had unwittingly set herself an impossible goal. She hoped to find her adult identity without forming lasting relationships and without realizing the potential of her sex. April's artwork was a genderless form of creativity, and even as she believed she was a stronger person for devoting herself to it, she was strong only for having denied the nurturing capacity of womanhood.

The psychologist Erik Erikson coined the term "generativity" to describe the highest achievement of the autonomous self: the ability to give of oneself as a parent. Yet for women, motherhood has too often been a first step after adolescence that occurred before self-awareness. Now a generation of women like April have mistaken motherhood—and even womanhood—for selflessness, deliberately stunting their capacity for intimacy and turning what should have been a limited period of solitary self-seeking into a lonely life's work.

But for other Self-Seekers, outright rejection of the old female models was impossible. As we shall see in the following chapters, these women struggled year after year with the contrary images of womanhood the Control Generation grew up with, vacillating between romance and independence in an unsteady quest for the self-confidence they should have learned in childhood. Instead, women like the Heroine, Laurie MacVey, had learned a quite different lesson.

5 § The Heroine: Laurie MacVey

"I always imagined I'd lead a very thrilling, tempestuous life. I would be a heroine like Cathy in Wuthering Heights *and I would have a Heathcliff. I would dedicate my life to one wonderful man and follow him to the ends of the earth—or I would be this exciting, dominant woman who would ruin the lives of all the men who loved her."*

Running Through Life

When thirty-five-year-old Laurie MacVey left her second husband in Los Angeles and moved to Atlanta to take a job as features writer for one of the city's major newspapers, her first act as a free woman was to buy a condominium in a new singles complex. The purchase symbolized her commitment to a fresh start, a new phase of life which Laurie herself would command.

As I drove past the guard booth and into the compound one warm Saturday morning, I thought I'd taken a wrong turn and entered a country club. Laurie's neighbors, men and women both, were jogging in the streets, playing tennis on community courts, swimming laps in the outdoor pool or practicing their strokes on the putting green. Inside Laurie's condominium, a tastefully furnished series of white-walled rooms with white pine trim, I found a tall, lanky brunette in a running suit. Apologizing for her clothes, Laurie told me she planned to join her neighbors on the running paths as soon as we finished talking. She hated to let a day go by without getting her three miles in.

The veteran of two marriages, numerous cross-country moves, and a half-dozen jobs in the past decade, Laurie has more in common with her neighbors than athletics. With the millions of Americans of the baby boom generation, she has traveled through her adult years with considerably more motion than direction. During the three hours we talked, Laurie described a life of perpetual searching in which she had adopted a series of radically different roles in what seemed at first a random progression. Laurie spoke of her years as an army bride during the Vietnam War, as a swinger in singles bars, as an ambitious cub reporter, as a corporate wife—and finally her current incarnation, the solitary runner. With Laurie MacVey's imagination, even the most mundane of activities could take on mythical proportions.

"I found out about running on an assignment for the paper," Laurie told me, leaning forward in her chair, excitement lighting her gray eyes. "It was about six months ago, when I'd first moved to Atlanta. I was new in the city, I didn't know a soul, and I was very lonely and down on myself after my second marriage collapsed. I really felt I had lost myself, sold myself away in that marriage, when I'd had so many hopes for it! So there I was covering the Peachtree Road Race on a day when I'd been feeling just miserable. And I loved seeing all these individuals—hundreds and thousands of men and women—all running to improve themselves. I saw all this enthusiasm, and I thrive on that. It's like sunshine to me. As soon as I turned in the story, I went out and bought about six jogging suits and a pair of Etonic running shoes, and I've been running ever since.

"I love running," Laurie continued. "It made me such a different person! I had never been athletic, and I had always been a little ashamed of my body since going to a Catholic girls' high school. But now I'm discovering my own strength. And the best thing about running is that even if there is nothing else going right in your life, or if you are lonely or in a brand-new city, all you have to do is put on your suit and your shoes and go out there. You are all by yourself, and it's just like the way you really are in life. You are all by yourself and you're running down that path alone. But when you're running, and feeling strong and getting somewhere, being alone can be wonderful. I am not denying that I get lonely, but I don't feel desperate to have a warm body around anymore."

As I thought about Laurie's erratic life, and listened to her fight off loneliness with her convictions about running, I recognized a pattern common in other women I'd interviewed. It was the pendulum swing from joy in love to joy in solitude, from the fantasy of self-fulfillment in romance to the ideal of self-discovery in isolation, that kept so many women from making progress in their lives. With the zeal of the recently saved, these women fell in love only to feel lost, then escaped to a solitude that eventually became so lonely they began looking for love all over again. Torn between old and new images of womanhood in a world in which, suddenly, a woman could be anything she chose, women like Laurie MacVey ended up trying out one role after another, only to find they had come no closer to meeting their innermost selves.

Rebellion and Romance

On the mantel over Laurie MacVey's fireplace sits a large candle molded in the shape of a woman's head. Cast in startlingly human shades of peach and cream, and with a wick in its center, I imagine the rounded wax face must glow and flicker with an extraordinary intensity on evenings when Laurie, alone in her condominium, lights it for inspiration and a kind of spiritual companionship. For Laurie lives a life dictated by her imagination and fueled by enthusiasms that light up her face as she speaks of them as if with an inner flame. Like April Benson, she is a Self-Seeker, but unlike April she has sought her adult identity not by stripping her life of female roles but by trying them on one by one like so many sets of clothes.

The new demands of professional life made many of the women I interviewed so painfully aware of the absence of female models in the careers they had chosen that they had forgotten the models of powerful femininity available to them in childhood. Laurie MacVey was one woman who had not forgotten. Like April Benson, she recalled childhood as a time to be endured, but Laurie looked forward to adulthood as her chance to realize a multitude of youthful dreams.

"As a child," Laurie tells me, "I was excruciatingly shy. I was an only child, and I was just scared to death of my classmates and their popularity games. So I spent a lot of time home alone in my room doing my homework and reading. From an early age I was reading the Brontës and George Eliot and lots of long Russian novels. Those books really shaped my life! I never doubted that a woman could be both powerful and feminine. I daydreamed all the time about how marvelous life would be when I got out of school and grew up. I always imagined I'd lead a very thrilling, tempestuous life. I would be a heroine like Cathy in *Wuthering Heights* and I would have a Heathcliff. I would dedicate my life to one wonderful man and follow him to the ends of the earth—or I would be this exciting, dominant woman who would ruin the lives of all the men who loved her. I thought I would just run through life and then finally I would be worn out from so much emotion—and I'd live the rest of my days alone with the memories. Or I would reach some tragic end, like Anna Karenina, and throw myself under the wheels of a train because life was just so overpowering."

Growing up in Memphis, a girl with Laurie's dreams might have tried making herself into a Southern Belle. But, dismayed by the preening of her classmates in the Catholic girls' high school, Laurie began to form a more distinctive ambition. She would go to journalism school and become a newswoman. Like Rosalind Russell in *His Girl Friday*, she would be a single career woman whose skill as a reporter won her the ultimate prize: the admiration and love of all the men she worked with. For a Catholic teenager in the mid-1960s, such a plan was only slightly less heretical than leaving the Church.

"As a Catholic girl," Laurie explains, "I actually had to get permission from the mother superior to go to a secular school. She called me into her office when she found out I wanted to send my transcript to the journalism school at the University of Mississippi, and started grilling me about what did the University have that I couldn't find at the Catholic women's finishing school where all the other girls were going." The encounter provoked the kind of dramatic scene Laurie had been preparing for all her childhood.

"I told her," Laurie continues, still gloating at the memory, "that I wanted to get out into the world and find out who I am. She didn't like that one bit. She told me that the last place I would find out about my immortal soul was at a secular institution. But I stood up for myself, which was a scary thing to do. I was the only person I knew who was asking that question: Who am I? Now it's an old hackneyed expression, but at the time I thought I made it up. In those days, women knew who they were, by God. They weren't anybody. They were going to go to finishing schools and get married and that was it. I wanted something more, something different."

Laurie won over the mother superior only by signing forms swearing to the bishop that she would attend weekly meetings at the Catholic student center on campus. But once out of Memphis, nothing would stop her from pursuing her ambitions in the way she wanted. With her sheltered background, she felt practically like a foreign correspondent working on the campus paper at the height of the civil rights movement. "I went to one meeting at the Catholic student center when I first got to school," Laurie recalls, "but by the second week I was so busy that I just couldn't seem to find the time to go back. I was really caught up in my studies and in the campus atmosphere. I felt like when people were singing the song 'Free at last! Free at last!' that it was about me as well. I loved meeting new people from different backgrounds, and I loved my journalism classes. I was one of the few girls in a gang of serious 'newsies,' and we put out a very professional student paper that was read by the whole town. And I also discovered boys! I had never really met any before, and I went sort of boy crazy. But I was still a good Catholic girl, so I just dated and necked—and only with boys from the Catholic fraternity."

Laurie rushed through college, acquiring the pins of one frat boy after another, and still planned to apply for work along with the other 'newsies.' "Up until the end of my senior year," Laurie says, "I never thought of doing anything else besides newspaper work. I liked dating—I liked it more than anything—and I wasn't going to give that up to get married. I thought my life of romance would just keep going, only on a more dramatic scale once I was out in the real world."

But then job offers started coming in and, says Laurie, "I started to get scared. I had just broken up with the last of my college boyfriends, and for the first time I was really frightened that I did not have a man to hang onto and face life with. The heroines I'd read about always had a man waiting in the wings, and I didn't see how I was going to be able to be that kind of woman without anybody to help me. All of a sudden I really hoped that I could get married as soon as possible so I would have somebody to help me in this frightening enterprise of life."

In the summer of 1968, Laurie took a job with the *Kansas City Sun* as a copy editor, but lasted only two weeks. "There were some incredible power plays going on in the office," Laurie explains, "the sort of thing that I wasn't prepared for after the camaraderie in journalism school. And I saw right away that I was going to be caught in the middle. I really thought I was going to be fired if I stayed around—so I quit and moved back home to Memphis." For the first time in her life, Laurie spent a summer doing what her Southern Belle high-school classmates excelled in: working on her tan and man-hunting.

"It wasn't just that I was afraid of being on my own," Laurie says, "but it was 1968. I really wanted to be with a man. That was the only safe way I could think of to get close to all these frightening things that were happening with the war and the protest movement. Even working on a newspaper would have been too isolated for me. The world was changing and I wanted to be part of whatever was happening out there."

In times of war, a heroine needs a man to bring her into the action. And that summer, Laurie found the man who could make her a heroine: John Donnelly, a young Catholic business school student who had just received his draft notice. "When I married John," Laurie says, "I got caught up in it all. At the time everybody I knew was getting drafted and getting married, and it was a time of tremendous upheaval. People's lives were being changed overnight! John was in the middle of business school, but his draft board wouldn't let him finish. I met him at a time of our lives when we were both on the threshold of everything, and I think both of us were a little scared about what was facing us—by the world at large, the war, and the fact that our lives seemed to be determined by factors that were beyond our control. John was a strong, kind man whom I could lean on. But in other ways we were like two children caught out in a storm."

At last Laurie had found her way into the romance she had looked forward to since childhood. Here was a man to whom she could dedicate herself. The potential for tragedy made her all the more anxious to take the plunge. Here, too, was a way to get married without losing herself: as John Donnelly's wife she would be no ordinary housewife, she would be a war bride.

The Many Faces of Laurie MacVey

Laurie and John were married in late August of 1968. John was drafted in September, and for an exhilarating two years, Laurie followed her husband from post to post through the South and finally to the Middle East, living always with the threat that John might be sent for active duty in Vietnam. The tension lent drama to an otherwise tedious life on dusty army bases. When John's tour of duty was safely over, the couple wandered through Europe on a much-delayed honeymoon. Relieved at their narrow escape, they were delirious lovers.

It wasn't until the two returned to the States and John to graduate school at Stanford that Laurie began to miss the excitement of the newsroom. Once she was settled in Palo Alto, life as a graduate student's wife didn't give her the same kind of thrill she had known in a wartime marriage. By the early 1970s, Laurie was ready for a change, which came to her in the form of a new image to cultivate.

"I was really ripe for a consciousness-raising group," says Laurie of her first move away from the war bride role. "They were starting up all over the Bay Area, and I joined one on campus with a bunch of grad students and university wives who were also beginning to question the limits that had been placed on their lives. It was so exciting to have women getting together and talking about problems we'd all thought we were alone with. All of us came out of it determined to make something of our lives." At first the only change was in her ambitions. Laurie approached local newspapers with the idea of a series about single professional women. But as her articles began to be published, she grew increasingly restless at home, and wished for herself the kind of life she had been writing about.

Soon, along with the rest of the women in her group, Laurie began to want out of her marriage. "It came as a gigantic revelation to all of us in the group that women were thinking human beings with lives of their own," Laurie recalls. "Every one of us had given up something for the men in our lives. And I realized I had given up a lot. It had been my choice, but suddenly I didn't want to do that anymore. Eventually the free-lance stories weren't enough for me, the group wasn't even enough for me. I wanted to get out on my own. I wanted to live in a real city. I knew there had to be something better out there.

"The problems in my marriage had nothing to do with John," Laurie explains. "They had everything to do with my idea of being free. That was what women were doing at the time. They were being free—from everything. They didn't need to be married. They were going out on their own and they were doing things women had never done before, and that is how I saw myself. I just had to go out and find out who I was. None of us believed you could do that with a man around, with all the crazy demands that being a wife put on you. I should have done it all before I met John. But I was a late bloomer—all of us were. After a while I got so into the idea of me, and pursuing myself alone, that I just had to get out of the marriage."

Within a year of their return to the States, Laurie had left John for a junior reporter's job on the city desk at the *Los Angeles Times*. But leaving her marriage behind was one thing—and finding herself was another. Like many women new to the solitary search for identity, Laurie was swiftly taken in by new images of femininity—and contrary ones at that. "I saw myself as totally split," Laurie remembers of her early years in Los Angeles. "I couldn't reconcile my personal life with my work life. It was a horrible, continuing conflict. I wanted to be two things at once: a serious reporter and a swinging single."

Through the several years Laurie would later refer to as her "disco phase," she kept up a heroine's romantic quest under the strobe lights of L.A.'s discotheques at night, and a professional's drive for success on the job during the day. "At work," Laurie recalls, "I was very businesslike, very determined to do a good reporting job. I wanted to convince people that I was serious and that I could be taken seriously. I was absolutely determined to show nothing personal, to let nothing emotional get in the way of doing my best job of reporting the news. Those were the years when I was wearing pants every day to work—no skirts, no dresses, *ever*.

"But at night I'd get dressed up in my best silk dress with lots of ruffles, and a little gold chain and lots of makeup, and do my hair gypsy style and head for the disco. Every night was a birthday party! I was a good dancer so I would get asked to dance a lot. I loved being the center of attention. It was like a movie where anyone can play the lead. You may be worried about your career and concerned about where you are headed in life, but at night you're a star."

Although Laurie had left her marriage to prove herself as a professional, her old dreams of heroic femininity persisted, taking new shape in the singles scene. "I felt it was very hard to pursue my career goals and retain my sense of femininity at the same time," Laurie explains. "If I was working like a man during the day, I had to prove to myself afterward that I was still feminine and I could still attract a lot of men. I'd go to discos and I'd latch onto the best-looking guy in the place and dance the night away. Sometimes we'd go home together afterward, sometimes we wouldn't, but I had to know whether he *would* have. That was what was important. I had to keep proving myself, keeping my scorecard.

"When I got to work, none of that counted for a damn. At work I was just another person, and I was judged by what I had in my head, what I could do for the paper. I loved that, but I guess it was frightening to me. I needed my nights at the disco to keep me going, even though the whole time I felt this tremendous, painful gap between the girl who went out and picked men up night after night and the person who went to work the next morning."

Just as the gap was getting to be too painful, Laurie met Michael Gibb, a lawyer who would give her the lead in a new drama: corporate romance. "I met Michael at a party," says Laurie, "in a context completely separate from the other lives I was leading. I was madly infatuated from the minute I laid eyes on him—and the disco star just burned herself out. I had never been so crazy about one individual in my whole life. He was tall, he was handsome, he was powerful, he had a dynamic personality. He was romantic, he was attentive, he was charming, and we were constantly having witty dialogue, like something from Noel Coward. Our romance was what every little girl imagines her courtship will be like. He treated me like a queen. He put me up there on a pedestal—with my frosted hair, my permanent tan, my paste-on smile. I felt so beautiful! I wore lots of very feminine dresses and high heels. Nobody who knows me now would recognize that girl!

"It wasn't long before he asked me to marry him, and since I had done just about everything else, I thought I might as well try being a corporate wife. I thought it would be fun and exciting, and maybe I needed to marry a strong corporate man to fill the gaps in my life."

Although in her disco phase of hard play and hard work Laurie had failed to integrate opposing sides of her emerging personality, the role of corporate wife soon robbed her of what little autonomy she had gained while living alone. She found that the glamour of being a corporate wife was largely imaginary, and that she had settled for a marriage that resembled the limited one she had always sought to avoid.

"We married each other," Laurie says, "because we were two strong forces that ran into each other and just blew up—BANG! It was explosive, and at first that was wonderful. That was when I still saw us as equals—he was the lawyer and I was the journalist. But as soon as we were married, Michael started staying late at the office and spending more time with his buddies after work. I realized he put on a whole act to win me, and once I was his, I was supposed to take a backseat to his life.

"For a while I tried to make it work on that basis. In fact I was willing to do anything to make that marriage work, because I didn't want to fail for a second time. I quit my job and played housewife. I played the role to the hilt. I hired interior decorators for the house we bought, I joined the women's clubs the other company wives belonged to. But nothing I did helped. It was as if all the romance had gone into the courtship and then I found myself married to a different man. The corporation that I'd thought of as so great, and so much like a family, was just sucking him away. There was no feeling left in him—and unfortunately there was a lot left in me.

"All along I had been waiting for a strong, powerful, dominant man like Michael to come along, and when he finally did, I fell in love harder than ever before. I tried everything. I tried working and not working, staying home and going out. And in the process I left myself behind. I lost myself on a doorstep out there in L.A. I had gone from feeling the most exhilarated I'd ever felt to feeling totally annihilated in the space of just a few months. I was too devastated even to walk out on him."

Laurie's second marriage ended as abruptly as it had begun. Michael announced one evening he was seeing another woman. He didn't love Laurie anymore, he said. "I think it's the only situation in my life where I have been fired," says Laurie bitterly. "I felt like an employee of a corporation in that marriage more than I ever did a partner in a relationship. When I didn't work out—well, that was it. The pink slip!"

Heroes and Heroines

As we have seen in April Benson's case, the constrained girlhood of the 1950s could leave a void in women where a sense of self should have grown. In April, that void soon filled with the determination to reject the models of womanhood she was raised on, and eventually to reject womanhood itself. For Laurie MacVey, who was also educated in a tradition of female self-sacrifice, that void filled with a parade of fantasies which only led her further from the answer to her persistent question: Who am I?

Dreaming is an important part of growing up. In his stage theory of male psychological development, Yale psychologist Daniel Levinson describes a phase, bridging adolescence and adulthood, that is given over to "The Dream." In puberty, he has written, a vision forms in the imaginations of most boys, usually featuring superhuman feats of strength and achievement, that nevertheless helps the teenager to leave childhood behind and face the serious tasks of adulthood. Levinson believes that women suffer as adults because they have had no such dream. Raised to marry a man and support *his* ambitions, women are not emboldened by the youthful vision that gives men the confidence to take the center stage in their own lives.

Yet women like Laurie MacVey suffer not so much from the lack of dreams as from cherishing inappropriate and even conflicting ones. While the heroine the teenaged Laurie dreamed of becoming—be it Cathy, Jane Eyre or Scarlett O'Hara—seemed both more powerful and more independent than a housewife, she was still a woman in the traditional mold. The heroine held men in her power in a way no housewife could, yet her identity still came from the men in her life. When the heroine lost her man, she lost her happiness, her power and sometimes even her life.

Disappointed with her romantic quest, Laurie caught on to another dream: the dream of the hero. For that was the vision that came to her women's consciousness-raising group. Eager to achieve in the man's world, they chose a male example to inspire them. Lured from her first marriage by the Myth of Independence, Laurie set off for a quest not for a love that would confirm her identity, but for identity itself. She wanted to prove herself in the centuries-old tradition of knights and warriors: like Odysseus, she left love behind to test her powers in the world at large.

But even as Laurie believed such a quest was as much a woman's right as a man's, she could not shake the feeling that she had betrayed her gender. For, as Levinson suggests, within all popular fantasies lie the patterns by which men and women actually grow up and find their place in the world. No one who dreams really becomes a hero or a heroine. Yet our youthful fantasies stay with us into adulthood and help us to accept the roles men and women are required to take up in society. The fantasy that following her love to the ends of the earth gives a woman dignity and power only glorifies the choice women have traditionally made: to marry one man and abide by his decisions. Similarly, the vision of abandoned love and heroic achievement magnifies man's common fate: a life spent away from his family striving for rewards in the workplace. The basis in gender of our dreams for ourselves is so ingrained that, recent studies show, only when girls are asked to imagine what they might do with their lives *if they were boys* can they allow themselves ambitions beyond motherhood and a narrow range of helping or theatrical professions.

When a woman takes up the masculine dream of the lonely quest for identity, she may feel, as Laurie did, a nagging desire to prove her femininity. This was the anxiety that kept her in the disco, and that lured her into a second mistaken marriage. In her search for self-knowledge, Laurie MacVey became a traveler between male and female fantasy worlds, never satisfied by either. To be a successful professional, must she reject love like the male hero? To be a powerful woman, must she be a heartbreaker—or an Anna Karenina who gives her life to love? Ironically, both roles destroyed any possibility of intimacy. The hero's distance guaranteed loneliness, and the heroine's total devotion turned love into dependence. Laurie's romantic dreams prevented her from discovering her true capabilities as a lover, and from seeing her lovers as anything less than distant gods. Shuttling back and forth between ideals, she never stepped back from the imaginary realm into the world of real people and genuine emotions.

Along with many women raised to be submissive but who yearned for power and independence, Laurie seemed to believe that she could actually become one of the roles she chose—if only she picked the right one. Instead, she managed never to address the identity problems that kept her from finding a mature love.

Love and the Search for Self

Like many women, Laurie MacVey was caught between woman's traditional self-definition in love, and the new ideal of self-discovery independent of romance. Her vivid but contradictory fantasies of the heroine's love and the hero's lonely achievement were only variations on the choice so many women her age felt they must make between love and the self. In fact as much as in fiction, women's lives had so often been given over to others—to lovers and then to children—that once, as Laurie says, "we discovered women were thinking beings with lives of their own," many fled from relationships, knowing no other way to assert themselves. Yet for most women, solitude was painful in its own way, and often just as threatening to selfhood as intimacy. The single woman asked herself: Am I somebody if nobody needs me?

Erik Erikson has written that for men love relationships during the years of self-discovery in young adulthood rarely provide true intimacy. Instead they become part of a man's search for identity, permitting him to test out his emerging values and capabilities in a relationship. Only as he grows more confident will he no longer use lovers primarily for self-affirmation, and learn to give affection without fearing the loss of self in love. To some extent, as women take up the search for identity outside marriage, their early loves have become learning experiences as well. Yet Erikson's theory hardly accounts for women like Laurie MacVey, the perpetual commuters between intimacy and isolation, love and loneliness. For them, the struggle is not so much for self-knowledge as against the old myths of womanly fulfillment in love.

And Laurie MacVey had fallen for many of them. In her first marriage, she played Penelope to John Donnelly's Odysseus, ever faithful to her husband, whose own life was surrendered to the fates of war. In her disco phase, Laurie acted the coquette, a seductive Mata Hari who may have controlled her lovers, but who was herself controlled by an obsessive need to prove her femininity. Finally, there was the illusion that, as with Cinderella and Prince Charming, marriage to a powerful man would make Laurie herself powerful. Instead, Laurie found herself diminished, in her words "annihilated," in her marriage to corporate lawyer Michael Gibb.

Women have an added obstacle to overcome as they struggle to answer the question—who am I?—with words other than wife or mother. The progress they make alone may all be in vain if they turn to love always in hopes of salvation. The spirit of willing submission only reinforces the irrational fear that love itself must rob women of their individuality.

The capacity for intimacy is still the most obvious sign of healthy self-confidence. No matter how hard we try to convince ourselves that the ability to live alone is a sign of strength, for women like Laurie solitude is essentially a defensive position, a period of recovery that must one day be followed, not by the surrender of self to love, but by the knowing union with another that is perhaps the most worthy human goal.

For Laurie, however, there remained the desperate striving for self-knowledge in solitude. Fired from her second marriage, she looked for a safe place in which to replenish herself. "In the late 1970s," Laurie says, "Atlanta was just taking off—like a Roman candle. Things were changing, the city was growing, and from what I'd seen of it on my few trips back to the South, I empathized with Atlanta completely. I saw myself as being just like Atlanta—just starting to make moves and starting to open up and become dynamic.

"And coming to this city, where there are so many other people like me, has helped me to work on myself. I don't want to lose myself again the way I lost myself in L.A. I must have thought I wasn't much good—now I think I'm terrific. I'm taking care of myself, I'm building myself up and I'm stronger physically. I'm a good person, and it's taken being on my own again to find that out. Before I used to think that to be that powerful, adventurous heroine I had to have a man around to help me. I didn't see any women doing it by themselves. But now I see them everywhere— out running, at the office, in the restaurants downtown."

As she spoke, Laurie was tightening up the laces on her Etonic running shoes, anxious to get out onto the road. We walked out into the sunshine together, where the scene was unchanged except for the faces of the athletes on the fields and courts and paths of the singles complex. As Laurie set off at a brisk pace, I wondered how many of the other women there were running with dreams like Laurie's, tell-

ing themselves with every pounding step on the pavement
that they loved themselves, were caring for themselves,
were making themselves better in their solo runs through
life.

Was this life better than staying home and minding the
children? Of course it was: these women were choosing
their lives. For them lonely self-awareness was better than
the only kind of love they had known: total surrender. Yet
the choices Laurie and so many others made still seemed to
be the wrong ones, based more on clues from the outside
world rather than from the inner selves they tried so hard to
reach.

Such was the case with the Conformist, Kate Holloway,
whose life was nearly as changeful as Laurie's. Having rejected the guidance of her mother along with most traditional images of femininity, she followed the lead of a fickle
peer group as uncertain about the meaning of womanhood
as Kate was herself.

6 § The Conformist: Kate Holloway

"I've always known I was deeply conventional, but the world changed for us—and suddenly being conventional meant being a radical."

A Scrapbook Life

Among women of the Control Generation, a life with as many twists and turns as Laurie MacVey's was commonplace. When we rejected the old patterns of womanhood, anything was possible—but for most of us, nothing felt right. In the quest for identity, many of us learned to detect the signs that we had lost ourselves in love affairs, unsuitable careers or fad ideologies, but failed to recognize our own inner desires. The closest many of us came to self-realization was breaking away from yet another bad job, mistaken belief or unhappy marriage.

Kate Holloway was no exception. As with Laurie, her life divided into wildly different phases. Yet Kate's many moves were directed not by fantasies crowding her imagination, but rather by an internal homing device that instinctively sought out the opinions of her peers. She was not a faddist, but like the "other-directed" teenagers in David Riesman's *The Lonely Crowd*, she followed popular trends more readily than her own impulses.

At thirty-one, Kate talked as eagerly about her Vietnam-era past as if she'd been a veteran herself. "I *am* the generation," she told me early on. "I've grown up with it and every mistake we made, I made too. Every idea we believed in, I believed in too." And Kate had the documents to prove it.

Seated on the designer couch in the living room of her garden apartment in one of Boston's fashionable brick town houses, Kate and I flipped through her photo album, considering the many guises of this slim, dark-haired woman dressed incongruously now in the black turtleneck and faded jeans of an earlier era. There was a chubby, grinning Kate in the navy-blue uniform of a girls' prep school; a flannel-shirted Kate locking arms with a bearded man whose free arm is raised in a clenched-fist salute. There was Kate on the steps of her all-women's house; Kate in tweeds and silk in front of the Harvard Business School.

And then there was the Kate Holloway sitting beside me, eager for yet another change. Lately, Kate told me, she had begun to consider quitting her job with a prestigious Boston brokerage firm to devote herself to the man in her life. This was the real Kate Holloway, she assured me. But was it?

Searching for Rules

By all rights, Kate Holloway should have proved the merits of the women's movement. The daughters of a professional woman who, says Kate, "read Betty Friedan before any other woman on the block," Kate and her younger sister grew up with an impressive role model right in their own home. "But instead of making things easier," Kate says, "my mother's ideas about women were always a problem for me. I ended up competing with her for radical status, or living out her dreams of what she might have done if she'd discovered feminism sooner—or sometimes I would rebel by turning conservative." No matter what she tried, Kate felt she could never win with her ambitious mother, who prided herself, above all, on being up to date. And Kate looked increasingly to her friends for the guidance and support she couldn't count on from her mother.

She felt the loss of her mother's presence from an early age. As soon as Kate and her sister were old enough to be left with a baby-sitter, Mrs. Holloway returned to work in her profession, ironically, public school administration in Chicago. The family lived in a distant suburb, and the commute as well as the stress of the job left Kate's mother frazzled. "She was a superwoman before there was such a term," recalls Kate. "And she did it all at tremendous personal sacrifice. My mother became a very tense, inflexible person. She had so much to do that everything had to be very organized and regimented—from getting us off to school in the morning to planning our vacations.

"Even so, she was not reliable as a mother. She was great with theory, but when it came to putting it on the front lines of dealing with children, she was a total loss. I admire her as a working woman during times before affirmative action—it took a lot of strength and determination to succeed in a field where women taught and men called the shots. But she never felt she'd gone far enough. She told me once that she regretted having children—that she would never have had to go into school administration, and she could have had a *really* good job in business instead. She expected me to be sympathetic!

"Of course she felt guilty for having those feelings about us. To make up for it, she'd say she would come pick us up after school and then she'd forget or she'd be late. She didn't realize how important it was for a seven-year-old not to be taken to the principal's office because her mother was late for the fifth time picking her up. It always came down to us getting embarrassed, or getting the reprimand because *she* was late, and all the kids in our car pool would be mad at us too."

Kate believed she had found the answer at least to her logistical problems when her mother suggested Kate attend the liberal co-ed boarding school she herself had gone to for high school. "I liked the idea of going off to school," Kate says, "but I told my mother right away that I wanted a different kind of school. I really wanted a straight, all-girls, wearing-skirts kind of school, and I had already picked out Saint Timothy's in Maryland. I think my mother was shocked that she had raised such a conventional daughter, but she was free-thinking enough to feel she didn't have the right to force me to go someplace else. And when I got there, Saint Tim's was just great. At last I was in a place where you could count on classes and activities and clothes and friendships and just about everything to be predictable and pleasant. My mother had been sending my sister and me to experimental schools ever since nursery school, and I really felt I needed a place with rules. I was just beginning to get into all that stuff with boys and dates and makeup, and Saint Tim's felt like a retreat from the competition, a lull before the storm we all knew was coming after graduation. There *was* competition, but it was all fair and square, it all had to do with measurable things like intelligence and athletics, and I loved that place. I didn't even try to hide that later when I was part of the radical movement at Columbia. Nothing could make me change my mind about Saint Timothy's."

Believing she would find more of the same, Kate applied to another women's school for college. But soon after she arrived in New York City as a Barnard freshman, Kate went through a transformation so profound that only her fundamental desire for rules remained unchanged. "I went to Barnard in 1968," Kate recalls, "thinking it would be just another nice girls' school. But there I was, living right next door to Columbia University. All the people I met were getting stoned and talking politics. I was trying to get in some good basic academics, and within months the whole campus blew apart. I couldn't help but be caught up in it. Everyone was."

The impressionable Kate met leaders in the radical student movement, and was soon taken up by a group so militant she will not mention its name or the names of its members fifteen years later. Kate's boyfriend was the hippest of the gang: he wasn't even in school. He'd dropped out after the spring occupation of campus offices with plans to carry the student revolt into the streets. Soon Kate was spending more nights in his apartment than in her tiny Barnard dormitory room, and using her study time for target practice with the group's growing arsenal of guns on a

New Jersey rifle range. "I've always known I was deeply conventional," Kate explains, "but the world changed for us—and suddenly being conventional meant being a radical. With the beliefs I held then, the only course of action I could take was to drop out of school, which I finally did in 1969. At the time I thought I was never going back. The revolution was coming, so who needed a B.A.?"

Kate was careful to hide her militance from her mother, as indeed she hid it from everyone outside the group. But her mother couldn't help finding out she had quit school and moved in with her lover. "This time my mother was just as shocked as when I asked to go to Saint Timothy's," says Kate, "and just as unable to stop me. She was liberal about premarital sex, but it still upset her that I was living with a man I wasn't married to. There just was nothing she could say.

"I was glad I'd shaken her up a little. But I didn't do it for rebellion. I was making decisions by what I thought was acceptable to the world around me. What I was doing was just exactly what most of the people I knew were doing. I dropped out of Barnard to live with a man, but I did it for politics as much as for love. That was the way people were making decisions in those days. We all asked ourselves, Is this match politically correct? Is this action politically correct? There was right and there was wrong, and there was no in between. Everyone was always saying, 'Either you're with us or you're against us.' It took me a long time to move away from the group."

The Love of Women

And when she did, it was for another group, although at first Kate believed she was acting only to save herself. "One day," Kate says, "I woke up and realized I was living on top of a powder keg and someone was bound to get hurt. I got scared—I didn't want it to be me. But more than that, I realized I wasn't getting anything out of that life. Women in the radical movement were no better than slaves. We cooked, we mended, we fucked our men. We were totally used! I wasn't even in love with the man I was living with. So I just packed up the few clothes I had and walked right out of there and moved into a house with some women I knew who felt the same way. It turned out I was lucky—some of the group members were hurt in a shoot-out not long after. I felt I'd escaped with my life."

In the run-down West Side brownstone where Kate and her friends set up housekeeping, there would be a new set of rules. "We became notorious for not letting men into our house unless by very formal invitation," Kate remembers. "If a man came over for lunch, we got kind of antsy. One night we invited a friend for dinner and she brought her boyfriend along, and we didn't let him stay. We were all so used to cooking for men and washing up and cleaning up after them that we really wanted to do things our way. The only way we saw of doing that was to leave men totally out of our lives. We made up some very elaborate rituals. Most of us had been living in the most primitive conditions before—just a few dishes and pots and pans. But now we hunted for treasures at the Goodwill and in used furniture stores and really fixed our place up with silverware and china and nice candlesticks and linen. Every dinner was a real community experience. We held hands and said a blessing before we ate. There just was no place for a man around that table."

For Kate, the ultimate rejection of men was to take a woman for a lover. Lesbianism was the perfect merging of the political and the personal, and most of the radical feminist leaders Kate now looked up to espoused it. "If you love women then you are in revolt against male supremacy," wrote Rita Mae Brown in a 1971 essay. And in the popular manifesto *Lesbian Nation*, Jill Johnston advised women that any romantic involvement with men was a "collusion with the enemy. The solution is getting it together with women."

So for Kate it was an easy step to take. Once again, "everyone" was already doing it. "When I left the radical movement for the women's movement," Kate says, "the big thing was trying out sexual relationships with women. Becoming a lesbian was a political statement and a search for a community. Most of us felt lost and out to sea with men and with the world, and the gay community gave us a lot of support. At the time I saw the whole world as men against women, and women being undone by men, and I just didn't want to let a man near me. I gained a lot of weight. I suppose I was hiding from men behind all that fat, but at the time I was saying, 'Men are so sexist, all they care about is tits and ass.' I was trying to prove that women, against all odds, would love me for who I was rather than what I looked like. We all believed that women made better lovers because they were more accepting and understood each other better. Sex was easier with women—it was guaranteed. Women were softer and more fun, and at first I thought they weren't going to pull the same trips that men did."

When Kate met Emily, a co-worker in the women's health care clinic Kate's household had helped to found, her involvement with women moved beyond experimentation. Emily had just walked out on a disastrous affair with a left-wing college professor, and the two banded together in a love based in large part on the desire to heal old wounds. Emily and Kate's affair lasted over a year, during which the two shared a room in the brownstone, backpacked through the Appalachians, and even visited the Holloway family in Chicago. Kate was still trying to outdo her mother. "Becoming a lesbian was a further step into rebellion," says Kate. "It was an adventure—way out there beyond the pale of what was appropriate. In my family, my mother had always worked and always assumed her daughters would work. She was more a fanatic about that than I ever was. So when I got involved with the women's movement it was with the lesbian element. To my mother, that was even worse than dropping out of school and buying guns for the revolution."

Lesbianism offered Kate much more than the opportunity to get a rise out of her mother. As different from Saint Timothy's as Kate's Manhattan commune looked from the outside, the household provided a refuge from the heterosexual power games she had always feared as well as a predictable set of rules. Like many women, Kate had moved in with the first man she loved at a time when the accepted rule for relationships was that there be no rules. For a woman with little experience of men, the setup that was meant to be liberating instead virtually guaranteed abuse. Unsure of how to protect herself, or even of what role she would have liked to play in the affair, Kate found it simplest to give up men. For Kate and her new friends, learning to love women was a way of learning to define and love themselves. With every pro-woman slogan Kate and her comrades uttered—"Women are kinder, women are softer"—came the certainty that "I am kind, I am soft." For women who had dismissed all traditional definitions of womanhood, the exercise was close to lifesaving.

Yet for Kate, the respite from heterosexual politics could not last indefinitely. Her growing restlessness brought trouble with Emily, who found herself increasingly devoted to lesbianism. "I began talking to Emily about trying things with men," Kate recalls, "and I could tell by her reaction that I just couldn't talk it over with her. She was very threatened. I kept my thoughts to myself, but I started noticing things. I started noticing that everyone in the radical lesbian community was dressing like a man. They all were wearing their hair short, and they were wearing jeans and looking as sexless as possible. One day it just dawned on me that we were all trying to look like men, that was the ultimate far-out look in being gay. I thought, Why are we doing this when we're women? When what we're supposed to love about each other is our womanliness? Why are we trying to meet male standards instead of establishing new ones?

"Then I began to feel that free and accepting as everybody was supposed to be, I was being oppressed in a lot of the same ways I had been in relationships with men. I wasn't allowed to say what I wanted if it went against the group. I began to think that a life with all the hassles of being different because I was gay wasn't worth it, if there were going to be all the same hassles of relationships with men. I tried to bring this up once and there was this long silence. Someone changed the subject and I realized I was being censored. It was sad, too, because, once I started to disagree, I was being shut out of what had been a safe place for me, a second home. I could see that deciding not to be gay, which was already a hard thing to do, was going to be even harder because it was considered a betrayal and I would have to leave and be on my own.

"Finally it all came to a head in one of our house meetings. I had just come home from the store where I'd bought a pair of hundred-dollar boots with money I'd gotten for my birthday. They were just beautiful, not those chunky Frye boots, but very delicate, really soft leather ones. And I just walked in and said, 'Hey, look at these neat boots I bought,' as if we were all girls back in high school. Given the way most of my friends were living, that was a horrendous amount of money. And in those days no one ever dressed up. So the fact that I had just spent a hundred dollars on clothes was absolutely unforgivable. They spent the whole meeting criticizing me for what I'd done until finally I just walked out.

"It was the culmination of a long process of separation. And it took something really clear-cut like that to finish it. It was clear to me that I wanted those boots and I felt OK about buying them, and these people were really hypocritical. I was doing what I wanted to do and I felt OK about it, which was unusual for me. I was always very sensitive to what the people around me thought and for once I just didn't care. I really came away much stronger for it, after feeling the satisfaction of doing what I wanted and realizing that was my right."

The Esteem of Men

Still, Kate left Emily and the others with a feeling of emptiness inside her where once there had been a compass showing her which way to go. She reapplied to Barnard, but her first months back in school sent her into a depression. "I can remember sitting in the library and crying because I didn't have a clue about what I was going to do with my life," Kate says now. "I had to fill out dozens of forms to get back into school, and on each one of them I had to check off a code number—01, 02, on up to 99—with each number representing an occupation. The number 99 was undecided, and I always had to check off 99, which made me feel so guilty and upset. There I was, twenty-two, still a sophomore and still not sure what I wanted to study. My younger sister had already graduated and was going to medical school. And with my mother's example and pressure to have a career I felt just awful. I had begun to recognize a pattern in my life: I kept thinking I could make one choice that would solve all my problems, the way my mother and sister had, and then I'd try it and find out it wasn't right and have to give it all up. I was in despair because I didn't know how to keep that from happening again."

Kate began taking courses in economics, at first, she says, because it was "a good, hard science with discipline even though it dealt with human issues." But Kate didn't see that she was once again trading in one set of rules for another. She planned to go on to business school and pursue the spectacular career her mother had always wanted. "Besides," Kate says, "that was what women were doing then, going out and proving they could have careers. We thought if we learned to hold down a man's job we would automatically become self-assured and capable the way men seemed to us. I had friends who learned to be auto mechanics and construction workers for the same reason. Business was just another one of those exciting male careers. Strange as it sounds, studying business administration wasn't such a radical departure for me. I told myself that I would find a job in the public sector—and that I was breaking ground for women."

In her senior year at Barnard, Kate fell in love again, this time with a man. A management consultant with a national firm based in New York, Mark Stratton admired Kate's ambition—and Kate enjoyed Mark's success. When Kate won acceptance to the Harvard Business School, Mark agreed to move north with her, requesting a transfer to his firm's branch office in Boston. This time Kate was determined to keep the upper hand in the relationship, and she applied some of the assertiveness she was learning in her new profession.

As Kate recalls, "I told him, 'I'm going to Cambridge and if you really love me you'll follow me.' It worked, and we moved in together—but from the start it was a disaster. I thought just the fact he'd moved up with me was a sign of his commitment to the relationship. I didn't think I was going to have to *work* on it. So I wasn't prepared for him to fall out of love with me—which is what he proceeded to do." Mark began visiting old girlfriends on his frequent business trips to Manhattan, and he saw no reason not to tell Kate about it.

"The way I saw it," Kate remembers, "was that his masculinity had been hurt by following a woman. He had to keep proving himself with those other women—and I couldn't take that seriously as a problem. I thought it was *his* problem and he would have to change. I didn't give him any room for expressing the doubts he had about following me to Cambridge, about giving up the working situation *he'd* been thriving on. I remember thinking that we had made a commitment to this relationship and he owed it to me to love me."

But Kate scarcely had time to fight with Mark. Business school absorbed most of her energy, especially once she found out she was good at it. Her plans of going into the public sector faded as she discovered she could plot a corporate takeover as well as any man. When Mark moved back to New York the following year, Kate's head was so dizzy with job offers that the breakup passed almost unnoticed.

"It was like all the other phases in my life," Kate admits. "I just kind of let things happen to me. I was just jumping through whatever hoop was set in front of me next." And the next hoop was a job offer from a prestigious Boston brokerage house where Kate would be the first female associate. She had lost Mark, but she had won the admiration of a new group: the male business elite.

Taking a Chance on Love

Succeeding in business, however, turned out to be different from excelling in business school classes. As a stock analyst with responsibility for investment decisions, Kate easily completed the necessary research and calculations, but balked when it came to enforcing the results. "You have to have a thick skin," Kate says, "to go into a staff meeting with what you believe is right, fight for it, and then walk away with no hard feelings. I find it very difficult to take a stand, especially with men who I know are not used to taking that from women. I watch the way men do it, and they put each other down in all kinds of ways. There is always an undercurrent of hostility that I just don't like. I've been criticized for trying to smooth over tense situations, which in my boss's opinion takes away from the creative process. But I'm too sensitive. I get hurt by it. I take it personally when my ideas are under attack—I end up feeling like a lot of people at work just don't like me."

Out of a new form of peer pressure, Kate had landed in a job that regularly forced her into the situation she most feared: standing up for herself in a group. Worse, self-promotion seemed to be a requirement for staying in the group. Kate began to take stock of her life, once again recognizing she had made the wrong choice. "I didn't really stop and think whether this job was something I wanted to do," Kate says. "Taking the job had nothing to do with the work itself. It had everything to do with the money and the status.

"In whatever my living situation," Kate continues, "I made decisions by what I thought was acceptable to the people around me. Sometimes it was for radical status, sometimes for professional status, but it was never really risk taking. Even though it seems that I've done a lot of exciting, far-out things, I've actually been afraid all along to do what I want because I don't see it very clearly. If nobody else is doing it and the pattern isn't there, I don't know how else to make a decision."

Conformity had also played a major role in her romantic

affairs. "I realized," Kate says, "that I was always falling in love with people I wanted to *be*. I didn't necessarily want to be *with* them, I wanted to *be* them. All the things I liked so much about Mark or Emily or my radical lover were things that I wanted for myself: their confidence, their commitment to a cause or a profession. I started to think it was time I decided what I wanted for myself—and the more I tried to figure that out, the more I thought about getting married and raising a family."

Kate had begun dating a documentary filmmaker named Joshua—irregularly at first because Joshua told her he planned to move to California in several months to pursue his career. But the more she saw of him, the more Kate admired his individuality, his refusal to enter the competitive world of finance that absorbed her days. "And for the first time," says Kate, "I started to really give to a relationship. I thought about all the mistakes I had made with Mark, and how I had really tried to dominate the relationship. I didn't try to force Joshua into anything, but pretty soon he decided to move in with me, and it's been great. It's still possible that he'll want to move to California, but in the meantime I've been giving him the room he needs to think it through, and our relationship has grown just wonderfully.

"Some mornings I come into work late if we're talking, or if we want to stay in bed. My job is flexible enough so that I can do that as long as I still meet deadlines—and I realized that money or status is not going to be what makes me happy in the long run. What's going to make me happy is a relationship that lasts. I never thought I'd be saying this, because it's just the opposite of what I thought I wanted all along—to be a single, independent woman. But I began thinking more about my mother's life. There she was working all the time, giving everything to her career, and still she was disappointed. She didn't have many friends. The women she knew were very much in awe of her and weren't even sure they liked her. They've told me she was kind of cold, and she made them feel bad because she was raising two kids and having a career and running a household and maintaining this perfect life that only *we* knew wasn't so perfect. For a long time I really felt that I wanted to live up to my mother's example, and to make up for all the things she'd never had the chance to do. Deep down I'm very proud of her—but we've never been close. I look at her and I don't want to be like her. I want to raise children who will like me, I want *people* to like me."

A few weeks after our interview, Kate wrote to say that she had quit her job to stay home with Joshua while he made up his mind about moving to California. She expected that, with her résumé, she'd have no trouble finding a job more to her liking when her savings ran out. And for now she was delighted with the extended vacation, and the new freedom to immerse herself in a relationship for its own sake, rather than for professional or political gain.

For Kate, who had made so many past decisions by consensus, and who fell in love according to rank, dropping out of the work force for such highly personal reasons seemed a good sign. It has always been an important part of growing up to move beyond the codes of one's peer group. For the women of the Control Generation this has been harder than for most. Rejecting their mothers' examples, they were determined to invent womanhood anew; following the peer group seemed, for much longer, to be the way of truth. Yet the new code of independence worked against the development of the self-confidence that permits a woman to move beyond mere self-exploration to mature stages of intimacy and generativity.

Still, I worried that Kate had made the same mistake so many generations of women had before: moving from dependence on the group to dependence on a man. At thirty-two, Kate was just discovering what once had been the accepted female virtues—patience, caring, compromise—and had given herself over to them as fully as if she were a teenaged bride. I couldn't imagine this new choice would satisfy her any longer than the others—or that this affair could end any way but badly, since Kate had once again dedicated herself to a man who was not ready for commitment.

The women of the Control Generation spent much of their third decade warding off the caring impulses they had seen their mothers give themselves up to. The Self-Seekers tried virtually everything their mothers had not—careers, sexual escapades, political protest—hoping to find in the world outside the heart confirmation of the selves they had been denied since girlhood. Yet the rejection of caring helped create the inner void into which rebellion, fantasy and conformity spread, dominating the lives of women like April Benson, Laurie MacVey and Kate Holloway, and preventing them from growing up. We may avoid intimacy, fearing its hold over us, yet in doing so we learn little about managing emotion. Kate, I felt, was in danger of being overwhelmed, even of returning to the housewife role her own mother had rejected.

Perhaps it was only inevitable that Kate, who was raised to meet high standards of achievement, would in the end choose a life whose highest value was the loving acceptance she had missed as a child. Or perhaps she was only rebelling once again by "turning conservative." Yet her urge to revive the qualities that once defined womanhood was shared by most of the women I interviewed. These women sensed their perpetual wandering might end if they could find an alternative to the Myth of Independence: a vision of womanhood that combined old and new, strength and vulnerability, autonomy and interdependence. Yet they simply did not know how to love without losing themselves, or how to give without giving in. Ironically, the crisis of female identity, brought about by ambitious women eager to write themselves new roles, was to center on the capacity for loving and caring that had been woman's undisputed strength for centuries.

PART IV
Caretakers

Female emotional "talents" must be viewed in terms of the overall price exacted by sexism. Much of our submissive, conciliatory, compassionate, and seductive behaviors have been cultivated in order to avoid either the fact or the onus of rape.

—Phyllis Chesler, Women and Madness, 1972

At the height of the women's liberation movement in the early 1970s, popular feminist writers like Phyllis Chesler began to promote the theory that even the most personal relations between men and women were infected with the disease of sexism. The qualities that characterized a woman in love—her generosity of spirit, her understanding and sympathy, even her desire—were no more than manifestations of the slavish dependence on men she was forced into by a male-dominated society. Germaine Greer wrote in *The Female Eunuch* that a wife's reliance on her husband for economic support kept her in a perpetual state of childishness, forever unable to realize her potential as a worker, as a lover, as a human being. In *The Female Eunuch* the traits of conciliation and compassion once again came under fire as the female equivalent of Uncle Tomism. Love itself was branded an advertising gimmick intended to lure women into the sexual slavery of marriage. Greer recommended that women seeking liberation refuse to marry. Only then could we acquire the aggressive energy that was thought by these writers, themselves admirers of male power, to be the only key to unlocking woman's hidden selfhood.

It was a time for halting the accepted progress of a woman's life. The once inevitable phases of marriage and motherhood were abandoned by women unwilling to develop the now suspect "talents" of love and nurturance. "The plight of mothers is more desperate than that of other women," wrote Greer, encouraging women to give up the last power they retained as a birthright. In the popular book *My Mother/My Self* Nancy Friday publicized her own early abortion and subsequent decision to remain childless in order to shrug off the legacy of "weakness" she believed had been passed from mother to daughter through the ages. In this atmosphere of wholesale reform, a generation of women, the Control Generation, grew up distrusting, as the Loner April Benson did, the men who might make them mothers. Worse still, they had learned to distrust their own compassionate selves.

Was it necessary for us to reject love, commitment and the oldest womanly talent of all—nurturance—in order to discover our strengths? As I heard tales of the Self-Seekers' floundering attempts to find themselves *by* themselves—continuing to believe in the half-truth that woman's compassion was a weakness responsible for her second-class status—I could only feel sorry that what had begun as a movement for liberation had in the end turned so many women against themselves. In every city I visited, single women were asking in desperation, What should I do next? Adrift without attachments to men or children, they wanted another agenda, a new feminist program to reassure them that their choices for singlehood over marriage, for work over love, were still the right ones. Who would tell these women to stop looking outside themselves and start looking into their hearts?

In my travels, I met a number of women I began to think of as Caretakers. These were women who had gone beyond the simple repression of emotion of the Self-Seekers to channel their compassionate selves into professions or into parenthood. These women were doctors, social workers and single mothers who had learned from an early age to restrict their capacity for empathy. Often the children of bitterly unhappy marriages, these women were strong-willed survivors who believed they could find a better life for themselves by confining their personal relationships; they cared for others only in exchange for a paycheck, or when in total authority as a single parent. Admirable in many ways, the Caretakers were also, deep down, more troubled than many of the women I spoke with. For, believing they had all the answers, they had stopped searching and did not know how to manage the doubts that had begun to sneak across the borders into their tightly guarded lives.

In her 1980 book *Unfinished Business*, Maggie Scarf wrote that women are more prone to depression than men because of the greater importance of relationships in their lives. Women suffer more at all times when relationships are strained or destroyed: when they leave daughterhood for adulthood, confront divorce or the death of a loved one. More recently, the psychologist Carol Gilligan has constructed a model of healthy female development on the same premise. Women, she writes in *In a Different Voice*, are the weavers of society's fabric, the protectors of the essential connections between people. Woman's fundamental capacity is for caring for others, one she learns from her mother and perfects over time as her ties to others grow and deepen. Gilligan even favors the old formula that women find themselves through love—so long as they don't abandon themselves to it as well.

The women of the Control Generation expected to thrive even as they denied the importance of relationships and suppressed the emotions that would create and support them. But it was not to be so. The Caretakers, like Dr. Beth Phillips, were finding that out the hard way.

7 § The Live-In: Beth Phillips

"I remember feeling happy when my boyfriend asked me to marry him—because I knew I had the power to say no."

When Change Is Unexpected

I met Beth Phillips late one evening in the deserted cafeteria of the Chicago hospital where she is a resident in obstetrics. Her long blond hair twisted into a knot at the nape of her neck, and her hazel eyes staring into the Styrofoam cup of coffee she was drinking to stay awake for night duty, Beth spoke haltingly of a crisis in her personal life that her busy schedule had kept her from taking in until now. When I arranged the interview the previous month, Beth had been living contentedly with her boyfriend of five years, Jeff Kaufman, a resident in radiology at a neighboring hospital. Just last week, however, Jeff gave Beth the alarming news he was moving out. He'd fallen in love with another woman, one of the nurses on his floor.

Strangely, Beth told me she wasn't angry with Jeff for his betrayal. But I sensed she was trying hard to rein in her emotions as she explained that Jeff had simply exercised an escape clause in the verbal contract that had kept the couple together for five years. "We had a commitment," Beth said, "but we didn't want to make unreasonable demands on each other either. We didn't want to go stale the way our parents had, so we had an agreement that if one of us felt strongly attracted to someone else, we should follow it up. But that was just a contingency plan that I thought would never come into effect. I thought it gave us the freedom we needed to keep our feelings for each other spontaneous."

But the live-in relationship Beth went on to describe sounded far from spontaneous, although in her troubled features I could see she mourned it more deeply than she would permit herself to say. "We got along so well," Beth emphasized. "From the day we met in medical school, we were together every night except when we were in the hospital. When we started living together it was very easy. There were no hassles about who would do what around the apartment. It was fifty-fifty all the way. All these years I thought we had what we both wanted. There were nights when we'd be sitting together, reading by the fire after a long day at work, and I'd think to myself, This is all I ever want from life. This is happiness."

Beth seemed most troubled by the news that Jeff was considering marriage. This was a real betrayal. "It came as a real shock when he told me he wants to marry her," Beth said, "because we always agreed that marriage wouldn't give us anything more than we already had. I asked him why marriage, and he said, 'Because she needs me and I need her.' It shook me up to hear that. I wished I could say to him, 'Jeff, *I* need you too, I want *you* to need me.' But that wasn't part of our language. I was always afraid of what it would do to us to admit we needed each other. I thought we'd become dependent and things would turn sour between us. And now it's too late."

As we talked, I realized that, despite Beth's reasoned acceptance of the situation, the breakup had shaken her deeply—not just with the loss of Jeff, but with the loss of a good deal she had believed in. Now she was beginning to feel things and want things she had steeled herself against for years, and the process was frightening. "I'd always believed that cohabitation was as secure as any marriage," Beth said slowly, "and gave a lot more independence. But now I think there may have been feelings I never experienced—and obviously there were things that Jeff needed and couldn't ask for because we never really trusted ourselves. We could never say to each other, 'Please do this *for me*. I want to depend on you for this.' Even something as simple as doing the laundry—we always did our clothes separately so that neither of us would take advantage of the other.

"I've always hated the caretaker role—picking up after people, cooking for people, or reminding people to do their chores, the stuff that keeps a wife locked in her kitchen all day. But I realize now that meant I could never be generous. Neither of us could. We were always watching to make sure everything was fair and square. On the outside it looked like we were the ideal couple, but we were actually playing our own little power game—and the name of the game was 'Who needs who less?'"

Like many women of her generation eager to avoid the stultification of marriage as they had seen it in their parents' lives, Beth had never learned that a mature dependence allows a relationship to grow. Without that trust, Jeff's and Beth's energies had gone into squaring accounts that, as time wore on, seemed only to measure how little the two had come to mean to each other. Now Beth had begun to worry about the distrust of caring that had affected every choice she made since leaving the childhood home she so hoped to avoid duplicating. Even her work as an obstetrician, with its evident caretaking responsibilities, had begun to trouble her.

"I used to boast," Beth told me, "that I just delivered babies—I didn't know how to care for them. And I didn't want to know. It was a thrill to be able to take charge in a situation where everyone else was so emotional and frightened. *That* was what I liked about the deliveries. I wasn't interested in what happened to the families afterward. I don't feel so proud of that anymore. I look at these tiny infants I've helped bring into the world, and at the nurses and mothers and fathers laughing and cooing, and I realize that all this time I've been afraid. Afraid of what caring too much can do to people."

The Noble Experiment

In the early 1970s, when unmarried couples still had to lie to parents, landlords and other tenants in order to rent apartments, and when wearing fake wedding rings and playing elaborate telephone games when relatives called were part of the package, living together *was* liberating. Sharing an apartment gave young couples the chance to know each other in all the ways young marrieds never had until after exchanging vows. Perhaps more important, co-habitation allowed women to enter a serious relationship with a man on an equal footing. If she was not a wife, and if she paid an equal share of the bills, a woman could expect the same privileges—sexual, domestic and professional—as her man. For cohabiting couples, the arrangement put an end to the double standard; the lack of a marriage license, contrary to their parents' worries, often gave women greater power in the early stages of romance than if they had been married.

After singleness, cohabitation is the second most popular social experiment devised by the Control Generation. In the early 1970s, there was not even a census category for such couples. Now they number well over a million, and "cohabitation" has become an official term used by social scientists and demographers. Of the forty single women I interviewed in 1981, seven were living with men and had no intention of marrying them. But by the 1980s, the initial freedom of living together had turned to something quite different, and the new power women held in such relationships had begun to corrupt. Like Beth, each of these women had made commitments to their lovers, promising everything from fidelity to household financing. Yet the connection between singleness and cohabitation was all too strong in their minds. Publicly part of a couple yet single at heart, the Live-In began to suffer from unexpected strains in her liberated household.

The live-in relationship evolved for the sake of women like Beth who wished to pursue careers yet believed marriage would keep them from their ambitions. Cohabitation seemed a neat way of combining intimacy and career for these women who still found closeness threatening to their autonomy. Yet, like Beth, many of these women had carried full-fledged cases of fear of intimacy right into their "committed" relationships. And since appearances indicated otherwise, the Live-In rarely had to confront the problem until disaster struck. By then, as with Beth, it usually seemed too late to change.

For many women, the advantages of living together had diminished to a simple list of the negatives of marriage. "Marriage wouldn't make me feel any more secure," said one woman who reported that her parents' and most of her friends' marriages had ended in divorce. Others were relieved to keep their names without hassle, to steer clear of in-laws and to enjoy the greater respect accorded single women at work. Near the end, Beth had developed an almost desperate dedication to the unwed state. "I didn't want to be a wife," Beth told me firmly. "I wanted to be Beth Phillips. I thought marriage would change that. To me, marriage means falling into the classic, stereotypical role of the woman as the weaker sex, the woman as the perpetual accommodator. I thought that if I didn't get married I wouldn't have to worry about that."

But instead Beth had fallen into the trap of labeling a woman's compassionate nature "weak." She had learned to despise those qualities that both men and women must bring to a relationship in order for love to grow and thrive. And Beth had settled for a vision of domestic happiness— the fireside scene—as tame and stagnant as any marriage. In this same diminished spirit, cohabiting couples everywhere that weren't, like Jeff and Beth, splitting up, began seeking help. Despite their relatively small numbers, co-habitants constituted 10 percent of the clients of couples counselors in New York and California in 1977, and by one estimate as many as 25 percent in Boston in the early 1980s. Like Beth, Live-Ins everywhere wanted to know how they had reached this impasse—and how they could change.

Like Father, Like Daughter

Beth Phillips grew up in a suburb of Washington, D.C., the oldest of three children of a prominent surgeon and his homemaker wife. Beth was her father's favorite, something of a surrogate son until her brother was born six years later. By then the pattern had been set: Beth was Dr. Phillips's preferred companion in his off-duty hours, accompanying him on his hospital rounds on Saturday mornings before the two headed off for an afternoon of tennis or golf. Beth's sister, Margo, was always the more feminine of the two girls, content to stay home with her mother, baking, sewing, or playing with dolls. As the two girls grew older, the difference became more pronounced.

Beth spoke of her childhood with the matter-of-fact tone she must have inherited from her father, the man of science. "I was always kind of a brain in school," she began, "but probably because of my father's influence I was always best at science and math. When I was in grade school, my teachers only knew I could read because I could do word problems. My sister was always the big reader, the daydreamer. I was the tomboy. I always avoided clothes that were feminine, soft and ruffly. I still do. Around the hospital I dress conservatively because I want to be taken seriously—or maybe I just don't want to identify myself with that classic, female, soft, ruffly way of being."

Beth continued to resist the outward signs of traditional femininity through adolescence. "My life came to a major turning point on just this issue," says Beth. "In elementary school I had been president of my class. The other kids didn't seem to mind that I was a tomboy and a brain. But when I got to junior high, I ran for class treasurer. My father and I stayed up late the night before elections to write my speech, and we both thought it sounded just great. We actually used rhetorical strategies from *The Selling of the President*. Anyway, I got up in front of our class of five hundred kids and gave the speech and thought it was terrific. But then this other girl, my opponent, got up. She had bleached blond hair and a short skirt and white fishnet stockings and white lipstick—all the right clothes. I was probably wearing bobby socks and saddle shoes. And suddenly it didn't matter what I had said. The other girl won. I dropped out of the social scene totally after that. I didn't understand how that could happen—it didn't seem fair that they judged us on how we looked. And that seemed to be the new basis for everything. So I just withdrew entirely. I took shop instead of home ec. classes, and I buried myself in the science labs."

At the same time that Beth was retreating into the orderly world of science, her parents' marriage was falling apart. Beth was already aware of her parents' different emotional styles, in part because she preferred her father's detached professional manner. Her mother's passionate outbursts over her father's long hours at work and weekends on the golf course reminded Beth of the flighty girls at school. "My father's attitude in the family was 'peace at any price,'" Beth recalls. "But for Mom, the only way she knew to get attention was an extreme show of emotion. It became exaggerated to the point where my father just wasn't talking. He wasn't home much and my mother was hysterical practically every time he walked in the door. She was very, very dependent on him, always wanting more of his time, but she was turning him away. My mother had retreated from the wider world into their marriage and her children. My father was her lifeline—emotionally, physically, intellectually, every possible way. That kind of dependence and possessiveness ruined their marriage and made a strong impression on me. I hated her for it."

For years afterward, Beth believed she had learned an object lesson in the dangers of emotional dependence and the foolishness of open declarations of love or need. As Dr. Phillips pulled away from his wife, he kept his less demanding daughter by his side. In her loyalty to her father and anger with her mother, Beth failed to see that the workaholic Dr. Phillips had also played a part in the collapse of the marriage—and that perhaps her mother was asking for time and attention she deserved.

In the end, both women lost Dr. Phillips. He moved to Washington, taking an apartment close to the hospital, and Mrs. Phillips turned on Beth with the anger and possessiveness she had previously reserved for her husband. Mother and daughter channeled their feelings of loss and rejection into a seemingly endless battle. As Beth tells it: "My mother and I began to fight all the time—over everything. Both of us wanted to be in control of me, and I was old enough by then so that she couldn't have her way. I knew what I wanted to do with my life. I wanted to study to be a doctor. But she wanted me to go out on dates, to dress up, to 'take care of myself,' she called it. What a joke! All I could see that leading to was a life exactly like hers, stuck in a house in the suburbs with nothing to do but interfere with her children's lives." Not only did Beth believe that her mother's behavior had destroyed the marriage, but she was beginning to see marriage itself as the destructive force, turning women into little more than meddlesome servants.

Looking for clues to avoid her mother's fate, Beth continued to emulate her father's style. She worked long hours in the science labs after school, visited her father at his hospital on the weekends, and applied to Yale, her father's college, over three hundred miles away from her mother and the D.C. suburbs. If her father could leave home, so could Beth.

Making plans for a career of her own seemed to Beth such a sensible solution that even today she has little understanding of her mother's plight. "I'm only sympathetic up to a point," she says. "You didn't have to do what she did. It's not good enough for her to say, 'I couldn't have done it any other way.' She wasn't in jail! There were women in her generation who had careers. She was bright and she went to college and she was exposed to other things. I get angry when she tries to claim she was the victim. I have a lot of trouble understanding how any sane person could get into a situation like that. She married my father just seven months after they met, and turned herself over to him completely after they'd seen each other only on occasional weekends.

What a crazy way to make such an important decision!"
Beth planned to manage her own personal life quite differently.

A Sentimental Education

At Yale in the early 1970s, Beth met the second most important man in her life, after her father. Terry Simon was
an upperclassman in biochemistry, whose brilliance in his
undergraduate work had won him praise from professors
and popularity among the new co-eds on campus. "Terry
showed me for the first time what serious scientific research
was all about," Beth recalls. "His enthusiasm was infec-
tious, and when we started sleeping together, it was part of
the incredible energy we were putting into our work. He
was a mentor to me, intellectually, sexually and emotionally. Meeting Terry was a real liberation, and I'm still
grateful to him for that."

With meeting Terry came Beth's first chance to prove
there could be another kind of relationship between men
and women than the dependent marriage her parents had
known. Even at nineteen, she was looking for more than a
good time from Terry Simon, although she was careful not
to tell him that. In her imagination she pictured herself and
Terry as two intellectual superstars whizzing about the
campus from science lab to dormitory with an energy that
would sustain the relationship even though the couple early
on agreed to make no long-range commitment. Obligations
of any sort seemed to Beth, given her mother's example, a
sure way to ruin any love affair.

Since coming to Yale, where competition for acceptance
to medical schools was fierce, Beth had decided to specialize
in obstetrics and gynecology, and went to work as a volun-
teer in a nearby Planned Parenthood clinic. She became
devoted to the idea of helping women to control their reproductive lives. It was all part of her desire to prove her
mother wrong: women didn't have to wind up in the suburbs with three kids and no job. As her plans took shape,
Beth never hid her ambitions from Terry, never spent the

night with him if she had exams the next day and vowed to attend whatever medical school she got into no matter whether it would take her away from Terry or not. She was careful not to let her feelings for him interfere with her own plans. She was certain that in the end her independence would win her his heart as well as his respect.

As a result, she was shocked to hear from a friend that Terry was sleeping with another woman on the nights Beth worked at the clinic or stayed in her room to study. "We had discussed the issue of monogamy," Beth says, "and neither one of us wanted to put that burden on the relationship. We agreed that we could sleep with other people as long as we were honest about it. But I thought we had this great, free relationship that would go on and on because we were two such exciting people, we just wouldn't need anybody else. I thought only married people would need to have affairs. Somehow I thought if we weren't married, the whole problem would never come up—we were free, so we wouldn't need to test the limits."

But Terry seemed bound to test them all the same. Not only had he been sleeping with another woman, he hadn't told Beth about it. Citing their one agreement, Beth used his dishonesty, rather than his infidelity, as an excuse to break off the relationship that, like her later crisis with Jeff, had suddenly released feelings in her that Beth feared almost as much as she feared marriage. She had expected that an open relationship would prevent the deeper feelings of need and dependence that she believed weakened a woman in love. She would cut off the affair before it provoked her any further.

"Of course I knew right away that I didn't like him sleeping around," Beth says, "but I didn't like not liking it, because then I found myself in the role of the screaming female—like my mother was with my father. It hurt me that Terry was treating me that way, but I didn't like the jealousy I saw in myself. I couldn't ask him to give up the other woman, and I knew he wouldn't change, so I realized I better get out before I lost all self-respect. I told him I never wanted to see him again—and until he left Yale that spring we avoided each other like the plague." Even as Beth discovered the need for more rules in romance, she had not uncovered in herself the ability to ask for them. Change remained to her the tragic instrument of fate, rather than a process she and her lover could initiate.

Beth tried her best to forget Terry. "The first thing I did," she recalls, "was I started sleeping around. I figured if he could, I could. And I think that was good for me, proving to myself that I could attract a lot of men." By the time she was ready for another long-term relationship, Beth was anxious to lay down more rules, even though she was still firmly opposed to marriage. "By the time I met Jeff here in Chicago," Beth says, "I'd sown my wild oats. I was able to say I didn't need to have affairs, and make a commitment to a relationship. We agreed from the start that we'd both be faithful—and though I still had doubts about whether monogamy could work for a lifetime, I knew it was what I wanted for as long as any relationship would last."

Fortunately, Jeff Kaufman felt the same way. Also on the rebound from a college romance, Jeff wasn't even particularly opposed to marriage—eventually. Still, Beth liked the live-in arrangement that allowed her to maintain her self-image as a single woman in all but sexual matters. Says Beth: "When we first started going out, what I liked most about Jeff was the way he respected my work and my time. When we were together, we were together, but when we weren't that was fine too. No demands. It turned out that I was much more committed to my career than he was. In fact he decided to go into radiology so he wouldn't have to be on call as much. I liked that in him.

"When we moved in together at the end of our first year of medical school, there was never any problem about household responsibilities. I mean, of course, the place gets messy, and Jeff is basically less concerned about dirt than I am. But usually what happens is I say, 'Jeff, I can't stand it. We have to clean up,' and he does whatever I tell him. I admire our relationship. There are so many men who are incapable of taking care of themselves. Jeff isn't like that—and I wouldn't put up with it."

Now Beth was talking about the relationship as if it had never ended. I asked her whether there had been any signs that she and Jeff were growing apart. "Well," said Beth slowly, still stunned by the events of the past week, "there had been a lessening in intensity. I didn't feel the same passion I once did. But I thought that was normal. I was proud of the balance we maintained, and I thought that was what would count over time."

Beth could only reiterate her long-held belief that volatile emotions would destroy love rather than fuel it. She didn't realize that in working to avoid her mother's fate she had idealized the impossible: a love affair without intense feeling. It was little wonder that Jeff had fallen in love with another woman who could willingly admit her need for him and accept his for her. Like many women afraid of the powerful feelings that grow with interdependence, Beth had so estranged herself from her compassionate side that she failed to see how little she was giving to Jeff—and how little she was getting in return.

The Controlled Heart

Like many of the experiments of the Control Generation, cohabitation was devised to keep women like Beth safely beyond the painful depths of caring they had seen in their mothers. But instead, the Live-In had committed herself to a love that could not grow. The cohabitant's creed, that no relationship should be forced to outlast its time, sounded reasonable in the age of the 50 percent divorce rate. Yet the Live-In never learned to tolerate the inevitable strains of a long-term love. She had invented a relationship that would self-destruct when either partner wanted to change.

Women like Beth had witnessed their parents' overwhelming need for change in middle age, for more passionate love or for greater freedom. As their parents' marriages dissolved or turned stagnant, they came to blame marriage itself for preventing change. Even as they rebelled, Live-Ins shared their parents' belief that long-term relationships force couples into assuming fixed and ultimately confining roles. Yet only deeper compassion than the Live-In permits herself could provide the flexibility she sought in verbal contracts mandating openness. The Live-In found herself trying to sustain her love on the shallow affection and good-will of her first meeting with her lover. Inevitably this momentary passion faded to a "lesser intensity," the safe "balance" that Beth had once been willing to settle for.

Women like Beth brought a semblance of intimacy into their daily lives, but were actually standing on the sidelines of romance. Their losses in love were all the more poignant as they had believed only marriage would extinguish passion. Like many women who had witnessed their mothers' crippling dependence on their fathers, Beth had decided that if she steeled herself from caring too much, she would not be hurt in love. But instead she found love itself eluded her grasp. Beth found herself unable to win her first lover with her strategy of independence and, worse in her mind, unable to control her own jealous feelings for him. In her next affair, Beth accepted a stricter commitment, but learned no greater sensitivity to her lover's needs, or to her own.

Beth was right to see her mother's dependence as weakening her. Her mother was one for whom compassion had too long meant deference to her husband's will. By the time her own needs surfaced, Mrs. Phillips was both helpless and desperate, resorting to the angry outbursts of a woman who had learned no other way to make herself heard. Yet Beth could not improve her own life by denying the gifts of love and refusing to learn the tougher lessons of *inter*-dependence.

And Beth was beginning to see that for herself. "Thinking back now on the relationship," she told me as she finished her coffee and prepared to go on her late night rounds, "I actually had very little confidence in myself, that I could stay myself if we got too close. And because I was so unsure of myself I could never permit any compromise. We never found *our* way of doing anything. We were always taking turns, doing our share, and proving to each other how self-reliant we were.

"And I could just kill myself for this one. About a year ago Jeff proposed to me—and I said no, I didn't want to get married, which was a lie. I did want to. But I couldn't admit that I wanted to, not even to myself. Instead I remember feeling happy when he asked me to marry him—because I knew I had the power to say no."

There are a thousand ways to avoid intimacy. Women can choose a string of inappropriate lovers, bury themselves in their work, yearn obsessively for a man who will not have them. But perhaps the most difficult to overcome is when we have allowed a man into our lives and not into our hearts. The Myth of Independence tells us that by keeping our caring selves in check we will find new freedom and achieve more than any generation of women before us. Yet never acquainting ourselves with the part of us that forms allegiances, that gives without thinking of return or reward, leaves many of us on the outside of human relations. Like Dr. Beth Phillips we stand by as our loves form and crumble, and do no more than assist at the births of families, never participating in the re-creation of life through love. And, as Meredith Gray was to discover, there could be no substitute for love.

8 § The Nurturer: Meredith Gray

"It's social worker's syndrome—caring too much about your clients and never leaving enough time for yourself."

Burning Out

Setting up an interview with Meredith Gray in Washington, D.C., had begun to seem only slightly less difficult than meeting the President. But the more she put me off, the more I wanted to find out what made this over-scheduled woman run.

At thirty-four, Meredith is a child psychologist with a large clientele of troubled children and parents who seemed always to be calling with emergencies just when she thought she'd have an evening free. "I could tell them no phone calls after five o'clock," Meredith told me when she called to cancel a second appointment, "but I don't have the heart. It's social worker's syndrome—caring too much about your clients and never leaving enough time for yourself."

When we finally met in her tiny, scarcely lived-in apartment in Georgetown, Meredith looked nearly as overworked as she had sounded on the phone. With a long swath of auburn hair fading to gray around the temples, and a face worn from the constant expression of sympathy, Meredith seemed most alert in her eyes: lively chestnut ovals that shone or clouded as her mood changed. She sat cross-legged in the middle of a large couch as I listened from an overstuffed chair, the only other piece of furniture in the small sitting room. Meredith's real home, I sensed, was not here in these vacant rooms where she spent so few of her evenings, but in the downtown office she rented in a building shared by a group of like-minded therapists. I could imagine her sitting just the same way in the middle of her office floor coaxing a shy or rebellious child into revealing his fears in play therapy with the set of mama-papa-and-baby dolls she kept on hand. Meredith seemed a bit uncomfortable to be the one on the couch this evening.

But if Meredith had been difficult to pin down by phone, she was remarkably straightforward in person. "Frankly, I was a little frightened to talk to you," she told me right away, "and that's part of the reason I let all those interruptions put you off. I've been feeling for a long time that I need to make some changes in my life—but most of the time I feel too upset to talk about it." Meredith tried all the same, going on to describe a crisis that she saw affecting not just herself but most of the women she'd known since college.

"You see, I grew up in the generation of social workers," she began. "We were all in college in the 1960s, and we were all out to save the world. We grew up believing you take care of other people rather than yourself—and it hooked women in the same way motherhood did a generation before. All my friends now are social workers or teachers or community organizers, and most of them are burnt out from overcommitment. None of us has any idea what to do next."

Meredith told me that a sudden wave of materialism had overtaken many of her friends. "A lot of them are applying to business schools, or bank training programs," she explained. "They think they're going to get out of this by learning to be more selfish. They think that it's the constant giving of themselves for such low wages that's causing their problems. But I'm not so sure of that. I can just see all of us throwing ourselves into a new profession and burning out all over again. I don't think that's the way to look at what's wrong with our lives. But to bring up the *real* problem is just too scary for most single women in their mid-thirties. We can't admit that we're lonely, and that maybe we'd rather be using the female part of ourselves that goes into our work on the families we don't have.

"We've worked so hard to get where we are, to prove we can be self-supporting and secure in a profession. Most of us never believed we'd make it. Now we have, and we're suddenly asking ourselves 'Is this all?' I used to say, 'I love my job, who needs a man?' I thought men would only interfere with the really important work of my life. I couldn't conceive of a man who wouldn't be making all sorts of demands on my time and forcing me to make compromises. Now I realize that compromise is part of making a fuller life for myself. I've been as defensive as a lot of the alienated kids I see every day, and I've ended up just as isolated. The worst of it is, my job has helped me to ignore the problem for the past few years, since I always feel involved with people. But my kids grow up, they get over their major problems—and what do I have left?"

Meredith ended her speech, and sank back into the soft cushions on her couch. She had thought this all through many times before, I could see, and still the problems seemed to defeat her. Meredith was the first woman I'd met who had good words to say about what she called the "female part" of herself: the capacity to nurture that she had channeled into her profession. Yet even she had lived in fear of its effects on her private life, believing with so many others that intimacy would deprive her of more than it could give. She had become part of a generation of women who solved problems of choice by simplifying their lives to ultimately meager dimensions. If love might conflict with work, then choose work, the Myth of Independence said. And for a woman like Meredith Gray, that meant devoting her nurturing side to a profession in a trend that now troubled hundreds of women who once believed they could change the world, and now were struggling to change themselves.

Role Transference

In the early 1970s, social scientists invented the term "role strain" to describe the problems of women attempting to cope with the many new opportunities opened to them through the women's movement. The woman who played mother, wife and worker all at once, they theorized, had too much to handle. "Role strain" was responsible for the new wave of divorces, for the sudden rise in mothers deserting their families to prove themselves on their own, and of course for the frustrations of that new media heroine, the superwoman, who answered to boss, husband and children and rarely to herself.

Yet as the decade passed, observers of women attempting to meet the demands of several roles found that the initial dire predictions were wrong. In their 1983 book *Lifeprints* psychologists Rosalind Barnett and Grace Baruch reported unexpected results from a long-range study of women in their middle years: the more roles the better. Mothers who did not work and workers who had no families actually reported greater stress than the women who shifted from one role to another during the day. Women enjoy being useful in a variety of ways, Barnett and Baruch theorized, and profit from the particular support—whether from family members or co-workers—each role gives them in return.

Women like Meredith Gray suffered from the opposite of role strain: role transference. These women avoided the inevitable conflicts arising from playing worker, wife and mother—the time demands, the conflicting loyalties—but came up with a different set of problems they could not have foreseen. As single women transferred the emotions appropriate to motherhood or romance into the jobs or apartments or cities they had grown to love, they forfeited the emotional backup systems acquired by women who marry and bear children. Stress and even burnout became the inevitable consequences of making something as fickle and impersonal as a profession the emotional center of their lives. Yet often, women like Meredith found themselves devoted to a job that had grown so demanding they had little energy left to pursue alternatives.

Role transference was not just the province of social workers like Meredith Gray or doctors like Beth Phillips, although the helping professions provided the easiest outlets. Writers like Laurie MacVey put their sympathetic emotions into their news stories. The sculptor April Benson channeled her feelings about family into her art. Role transference was one of the teachings of the Myth of Independence. Said one thirty-two-year-old business school graduate, "The women's movement convinced us that the professions would satisfy our every need. We all believed we should keep working and keep looking until we found jobs we absolutely loved. Anything less was not enough. To say you didn't love your job was like our mothers' saying they didn't love their husbands. It was an admission of failure."

Role transference not only diminished a woman's social life, but often distorted it. Once a woman's emotions became bound up in her profession, romance could be viewed only as a sideline. The same woman who told me "I'm a better journalist because I have a woman's empathy for people" thought nothing of rejecting a string of lovers for reasons as trifling as their taste in clothing. Another woman, an entrepreneur who boasted of "making love to my career," described the men she dated in terms of their "perks" and analyzed the "downside" risks of involvement as if love were a business transaction.

Behind these defenses, of course, lay the fear felt by many women new to the professions that any deep affection would force them back into the role of housewife. The best way to prevent interference was to prevent oneself from caring too much about any man, an effort made all the easier when work became both lover and family. Some women, fearful of the grasp of husbands and children, claimed that a group of loyal women friends was all the "family" they needed. Yet these women inevitably grew anxious and even angry with friends when they heard news of engagements or pregnancies. The concept of *Friends as*

Family, as a popular book on the subject was called, turned out to be essentially negative as "family" members jealously pressured one another into staying single for the good of the group. The strategy rarely worked, and few alternative families survived many such crises.

For women, accustomed for generations to the merging of work and love in their role as housewife, role transference seemed the obvious way to succeed in a profession. So women "gave their all" to their work in a very different sense than did men, who have learned to live with a separation of work and family roles. Woman's greater capacity for empathy often helped her on the job, as it did Meredith Gray. But just as often it also helped her to value her job too highly at the expense of personal relationships. Role transference might have been a convenient adaptation to single life for women during a time of self-discovery preceding marriage. Yet for women like Meredith Gray, it seemed to demand rather than support singleness, prolonging youthful fears of intimacy first learned in the insular nuclear families of their childhood.

Growing up Too Fast

If the Live-In, Beth Phillips, grew up despising the caretaker role, Meredith Gray learned to play it from an early age. "Most of my skills as a therapist," Meredith said in her forthright manner, "were developed in my own family, where my role was to be the caretaker of everybody. That was my technique of survival. My parents had a very stormy marriage, and some of my earliest memories of my mother are of her sitting in tears as my father brutalized her, verbally. My father was brilliant and successful and charming, socially, but also very insecure and my mother was the only person who saw that side of him. And he made her pay for it.

"My role was mediator between my parents and protector of my mother and younger sister. To do that I had to be competent, I had to be as adult as I could as soon as I could. My father was very rational, a terrific arguer, but always on the wrong side. My mother was emotional and couldn't argue back, but she was on the right side. I would come in and take my mother's side but use my father's verbal tools, which meant being as rational as he was on an emotional issue. The trick was to act unemotional. If I cried I had to go to my room. I was reduced to upset child status."

Meredith's adoption of the caretaker role stemmed from a deep sympathy for her mother, again quite different from Beth Phillips's impatient dismissal of her "weak" mother's plight. "Somehow I think my mother could never understand how she'd ended up with the marriage she had," Meredith explained. "She was very beautiful, really recognized as a beauty in the circle of New Yorkers where she met my father. And my father was a successful trial lawyer whom everyone admired. They just didn't see his bad side, and neither did my mother until she married him. She was just twenty, she'd had an easy life and could have gone on to do any number of things, but she'd never had to fight for anything before. When she married my father and they moved up to Connecticut, he insisted she stay home and raise the kids. She lost everything she'd known, and spent the next thirty-five years suffering for it."

If Meredith became self-appointed mediator, her defenseless mother conspired to keep her that way. She turned her attentions away from her husband and toward her older daughter, attempting to mold her into the stronger woman she might have been herself. "We looked a lot alike," says Meredith, "and my mother always dressed me in a child's version of her clothes. But we both knew I would grow up to be something different. I remember very distinctly my mother telling me how envious of me she was because I would have a life of my own, because I could have the career she never had. She was also very much against me marrying young. She even got her doctor to prescribe birth control pills for me before I went away to college—she didn't want anything to stop me from living life on my own terms."

It was all too common, before the era of consciousness-raising groups, for women like Mrs. Gray to turn to their young children for support when a marriage soured. In the insular suburban households of the 1950s and early 1960s, the taboo against divorce and the social pressure on women to devote themselves to their children often combined to produce a peculiarly inverted relationship in which the child played parent to the mother. While Meredith now believes those years brought out many of her strengths, they left her bitter as only a parentless child can be.

"My mother's concern for my future," Meredith says, "was her way of making me strong but keeping me close— as if I were her other half. It was only through great strength of will that I broke away. As long as I was there to take her side and fight for her, she never had to take things into her own hands. I didn't see that at the time. All I saw was that she was the victim, she was treated unfairly, and someone had to speak up for her. Now I wonder why she never just said, 'I can't stand living this way. I'm leaving.' My parents had the same battle over and over and over, and she always lost, and she got to be more and more of a martyr. She really believed she was stuck—and maybe she was. The times were not very supportive for women like her.

"But, thanks to her encouragement, I knew I wouldn't have to live my life the same way. When I got to college, I had a life of my own. I was no longer running back and forth between Mommy and Daddy, and I learned to tune out my mother's efforts to drag me back into it. The only problem was, I didn't know what to do with myself. I had spent so much time taking sides in a fight that was really none of my business that I had no idea what *I* wanted out of life. The only thing I did know was that I didn't want to be a victim."

Leaving Home

While Meredith's early family role had given her the strength to take care of others, it also left her suspicious of uncontrolled emotions—the ones that might reduce her to "upset child status," or the fiercer ones she presumed to be hidden inside most men. The competence Meredith learned in childhood translated into inhibition once she was among men and women her own age at college. For her first years at Oberlin in Ohio, she had little reason to fear victimization from the men she was careful always to keep at a safe distance. And when she tried getting closer she would find she had a lot of growing up still to do.

"I really didn't know how to talk to men in a personal way," says Meredith. "I was fine in my classes, where I was never afraid to speak up and argue a point. But outside class I never knew how to make conversation. I told myself the problem was that men didn't like challenging women— they saw me as unfeminine and I intimidated a lot of people. In my senior year I got to be close friends with a boy named Brant who told me as much. I asked him, 'What is it? What do I have to change?' And he said, 'Everything. The way you dress, the way you talk, the way you walk. . . .' I was in tears. I told him, 'I can't change all those things! That's me!'"

But change she did. "My first and longest love affair was with Brant," Meredith says. "It's hard for me to believe this now, but I felt that he saw all this about me—how strong and intimidating I was—and he saw something lovable in me anyway. It was all inside out, but that's how the whole relationship was. He was calling the shots from the start, and I was trying my best to seem softer, more like his idea of a woman. Much to my surprise, and his too I think, I became utterly dependent on him—for approval, affection, my sense of self-worth. And I'm sure it made him feel good to think he had a strong woman wrapped around his finger.

"I followed him here to Washington after Oberlin, and we lived together for three years, which were some of the worst years in my life, after my childhood. We fought a lot, and I can't blame him entirely for that. It was partly because of my parents' example. I used to provoke fights just to have the intensity in the relationship. It took me a long time to realize that I didn't have to have something to disagree about all the time, I didn't always have to be fighting for control of the relationship, or for control of myself, which is what I was fighting for very desperately.

"I just could never seem to get my life going. All the dreams my mother and I had for a career seemed to be going by the boards. Brant was in graduate school in philosophy, and the only money coming in aside from his student loans was my salary as an aide in different hospitals. Somehow I knew I wanted to be in the helping professions, but in those days when very few women held responsible jobs, it was hard to know where to start. We needed money so badly I couldn't take time off to think things through. My ambitions were still very high, but Brant was always putting them down. Anytime I talked about going to grad school, he'd tell me I didn't have the staying power to go through with it. He'd always say, 'If you really wanted to do it, you'd be doing it right now.' And for a long time I believed him. I was so dependent on him for approval I really was stuck."

Despite her vow never to be made a victim, Meredith had, like many women, re-created in her first love affair the unequal balance of her parents' stormy marriage. But Meredith wouldn't play the victim for long. She had long ago learned to act on her feelings, something her mother could never manage. "I finally got so depressed," Meredith continued, "that I started seeing a therapist, and only then did I see how much I'd lost myself to that man. I realized that Brant was putting me down in order to feel better about himself, and I began to think about ways I could get back on my feet. My therapist was the first strong woman I'd met, and she made a very powerful impression on me. I started to recognize in her some of the qualities I'd once been certain of in myself and had been trying to deny. She was compassionate and giving, and yet she was always calm and reasonable. Partly because I was so inspired by her, but really because that was the direction I'd been heading in all along, I decided to go into counseling myself."

As with many women, the decision to pursue a career gave Meredith the courage to break off a relationship she had long recognized as self-destructive. As soon as she received an acceptance letter from a master's program in social work, she moved into an apartment by herself. The parting with Brant, she told me, was surprisingly easy, as if the constant warring had at last exhausted all their feeling for each other. But unfortunately Meredith came to associate singleness with self-discovery, and when she did, the habit of role transference, channeling all her nurturing capabilities into her profession, was set.

"From then on," says Meredith, "my whole life changed. When I started practicing as a therapist I found out that I was good at it. All kinds of talents began coming out, in spite of the lack of confidence I'd had since I met Brant. Therapy draws on the female part of me that's always been there, but that I didn't know how to use outside my family. Nurturing and compassion are good qualities that women have perfected over the ages—I have them, and I'm proud to use them. And I'm not going to let any man stand in the way of that like Brant did."

In Meredith's late twenties when she was setting up her practice, it often seemed she was just too busy to see any man regularly. There were long nights going over the new cases she took on, and even longer ones spent balancing office expenses against client fees as she struggled to manage her own business. "When I began to have a few evenings free," Meredith told me, "I went through a phase that a lot of single women go through in their early thirties. No man ever seemed good enough. One man's sense of humor was wrong, another dressed badly, another was too much of a sexist. It got so I could tell on the first date just what it was—and I thought that was great. It saved me a lot of disappointing second dates. But after a while I began to wonder why I was putting myself through the whole window-shopping dating routine. Now I've gone back to burying myself in my work and seeing my women friends on the weekends. I don't honestly miss men that much—but I do feel lonely. And it sometimes nags at me that maybe I didn't give one of those men a real chance. The first thing you learn as a therapist is to mistrust your first impression and wait to see what else emerges as you get to know your client. It never occurred to me to look at men that way."

Since leaving Brant, Meredith had only looked at men as potential thieves of her hard-won contentment. Like many other women, she had come to fear that all relationships with men would require the same sacrifice of ambition that an early love affair, founded largely on her desire to retreat from the challenges of adulthood, had exacted. In Meredith's case, the association of love and self-denial had a twisted result: she learned to fear men even as she gloried in her feminine qualities, the same ones that would have served her well as a wife and mother. In some ways Meredith had done no more than many women, dissatisfied with their men, had done for generations inside marriage: turn their attention to the nurturing of children. But Meredith's children were not her own. Role transference had left her caring for people who could never become a part of her family—and as ambivalent as any member of the Control Generation about the place of caring in her private life.

The Female Part of Me

At last, in listening to Meredith Gray, I had heard a woman of the Control Generation speak positively of her female qualities of empathy and nurturance. These were the same characteristics that Ellen Barnes, the Professional, had dismissed as unsuited to her work; that Lynn Feldman, the Feminist, believed made her a victim to men; that Beth Phillips rejected as signs of weakness. Even Meredith feared them in her personal life. What was this "female part" that caused women of the Control Generation so much anxiety—was it good or bad, learned or innate?

In the early years of the women's movement, research psychologists devoted themselves to proving that women could perform as well as men in a variety of situations from which they had traditionally been excluded. The unisex doctrine of the 1960s and 1970s ruled psychology as firmly as it governed dress and hairstyles. Yet as women began to prove themselves in formerly male occupations, researchers felt freer to explore differences, to ask the question "What makes a woman?" without fear of uncovering weakness.

Not surprisingly, it is the nurturing capacity that Meredith instinctively termed "the female part of me" that researchers have isolated as the thread that runs through women's lives, differentiating them from men, from infancy to adulthood.

In a recent study, the psychologists Abraham Sagi and Martin Hoffman played tapes of an infant's cry near the cribs of babies still too young to leave their hospital nursery, and found that girls scarcely one day old cried out in a sympathetic response to the recorded wails, while boys remained relatively indifferent. The team speculated that these cries were the early signs of woman's biological predisposition to answer the needs of others. In a 1976 study, psychologist Janet Lever observed children at play and confirmed what most of us recall from our own childhoods: boys prefer regulated games like baseball or football while girls favor social ones in which winning and losing are less important than conversation. Cat's cradle, jump rope and jacks are all talking games in which some girls may excel but no player need go away hurt. In comparing the way girls and boys resolved arguments that arose during play, Lever found that boys settled disputes by the rule book while girls would rather quit a game than argue a point. Girls would rather continue a friendship, Lever concluded, while boys preferred to continue a game. Concern for others was the chief feature of girls' play, part of their early training for a life of caretaking.

Studying a group of women in their late teens and twenties who were considering abortions, Carol Gilligan found in 1977 that this same principle of concern for others continued to rule women's decisions. A woman considering an abortion often thought of how it would affect her lover, her family, and of course the unborn child before thinking of herself. Most of the women, Gilligan discovered as she interviewed her subjects over several weeks, eventually learned to count their own feelings into the decision. But this too showed their fundamental altruism at work, as they recognized that if *they* weren't happy, nobody would be happy. Self-sacrifice was not necessary to care for others.

Yet empathy was so clearly the deciding factor for women in this important life crisis that Gilligan was moved to theorize that for women "care . . . becomes a universal obligation."

For women of the Control Generation, our problem is what to make of this trait in ourselves, this concern for others that sometimes holds us back when we want to play to win and yet is responsible for our deepest feelings. We have wanted to avoid the confinement, both physical and emotional, that so many of our mothers knew as a result of making caretaking their life's work. Yet we too readily believed we must reject motherhood and our "weakening" instinct for compassion in order to save ourselves. The Caretakers had learned to make use of their nurturing side. A woman like Meredith Gray could give of herself all day long, if she was certain of receiving a paycheck—our generation's measure of self-worth—for her efforts. Yet she could not spend more than a few evenings with a man without fearing that her compassion, when unmetered by the therapeutic hour, would turn her into the helplessly emotional woman her mother had been.

"In order to do my work," Meredith told me despairingly as we ended our talk, "I have to have a vision of what makes a happy couple and a healthy family. And I do have that vision: marriage should be a partnership, two people building something together, sharing burdens that alone are very hard to bear, and also making something that alone you couldn't have. But it just doesn't seem to work for me. I'm going to have to try harder, because my life just doesn't have enough in it right now. But I'm still very afraid of losing what I've already got."

When I met Carla Ramsey, I learned just how far that fear could take a woman.

9 § The Matriarch: Carla Ramsey

"I never thought childbirth was going to be the culmination of some serious romantic passion."

A Modern Nativity

"The winter I got pregnant," Carla Ramsey told me, "I had turned thirty-two in November. New Year's came and I looked back over the year and thought, I don't have what I want. If I don't have a child this year, I may not be able to later. So getting pregnant was my New Year's resolution. I probably would have chickened out except I conceived on the second try."

We were talking in Carla Ramsey's office, a spacious room with a teak desk, plush couch and armchairs in the Beverly Hills theatrical agency where she works, a short drive from the small Spanish-style bungalow she owns and shares with her four-year-old daughter Kyra in Santa Monica. At thirty-seven, with soft brown curls that ring a determined, full-featured face, Carla Ramsey was telling me what might have been a typical story of delayed motherhood for a professional woman—except that Carla was single at the time of her New Year's vow. "It was scary," Carla admitted, even as she displayed the same calm assurance that has made her a successful agent and competent single mother, "but it was something I'd considered for a long time. I'd thought of adopting, but I knew that would be difficult for a single woman. Besides, I wanted the whole experience. Why have all this biological equipment and not use it?"

Carla's story sounded even more unusual as she continued. "Kyra's father didn't know about my plans," she said. "I'd been going out with him for over five years, but fidelity was never one of his strong points. He wasn't interested in marriage or fatherhood. I knew that when Kyra was born that would be the last I saw of him. And it was. I told him, 'I'm pregnant,' and he said, 'Good-bye.'

"He quit his job and left town, though not before he went to see a lawyer about his legal responsibilities. It turned out I could have made claims in a paternity suit up until Kyra was age five. But I had no intention of doing that and I wrote out a paper saying so. Still, he knew that legally there was no way I could give away Kyra's rights. I think that's why he left. I haven't seen him since I was three months' pregnant, and I have no idea where he is, though I could find him through his parents if I had to.

"I was lonely during the pregnancy, but that was the choice I made. I always thought I'd get married sometime, but it got to the point where I could see that wasn't happening. It was now or never. I'd always been an independent person—and I guess I'd always fallen in love with men who liked that about me, which is one reason I'm not married. They wanted me to stay independent. I used to get mad about that, but there wasn't much I could do to change it.

"It would have been nice to have a man around, but I had plenty of support. My friends gave me a shower and sixty women came! They gave me things like a washing machine and two cribs—one for home and one for the office. And sometimes now, when I look at my friends and their families, I'm just as glad he wasn't around. It could be much worse. We could be divorced and he could be suing me for custody. My situation is better than that. I have a good income, I don't depend on alimony. I own my house. And Kyra never has to see any friction between two parents. She has my full attention whenever she needs it. And there's one thing Kyra will always know: she is very much a wanted child."

The New Matriarchy

In every city I visited looking for representative single women to interview, I heard about single mothers like Carla Ramsey. Other women spoke of these older unwed mothers with surprising envy as "autonomous," and "self-sufficient," often adding, "I couldn't do it myself, but I admire women who can." After visiting the homes and meeting the children of several such women, I began to think of the Carla Ramseys of the world as the ultimate products of the Myth of Independence that had first lured women out of their suburban kitchens a decade ago. The women truest to the values of the Control Generation, they were doing it all—everything!—on their own.

Certainly they were the front-runners in one of the most startling recent trends in American demography. In 1970, only a quarter of a million women were raising children born to them out of wedlock. By 1980, that figure quadrupled to over a million, a fact all the more surprising since overall birthrates declined during the same period. While the majority of illegitimate births were to teenagers, the birthrates for unmarried women throughout the childbearing years increased significantly. For the first time, a woman like Carla Ramsey became a census figure. In Southern California, obstetricians estimated that 5 percent of their expecting patients had no intention of marrying the fathers of their children, and often no intention of even living with them, thereby confining the male parental role exclusively to insemination. In New York City, a group of over a hundred such women in their thirties banded together in a lobbying and support group calling themselves "Single Mothers by Choice."

The single mothers I spoke with each emphasized that their choice to become parents was a matter of simple common sense. Like other women, they told me, they had always wanted to be mothers. Now they were. Like Carla, each of them believed she was giving her child care as good if not better than the millions more single women who suddenly found themselves supporting their families fol-

lowing the shock of a divorce. Some, like Carla, even believed that as individuals they might be giving more
constant and reliable support to children than a married
couple that suffered the inevitable strains of matrimony.

But their lives were not like those of ordinary mothers,
and their choice for motherhood was different from any
that had resulted in children in recent history. Even the
unwed teenager conceives her child because of some stir-
rings of love, first, for a man. While these "autonomous"
single mothers could rightfully take pride in raising their
children in households of emotional and financial security,
they had become mothers primarily for self-fulfillment. In a
1982 study of single mothers by choice, psychologist Mar-
garet Fox found that, when asked what they liked most
about motherhood, her subjects often answered selfishly. "I
like that she's mine," said one woman of her infant daughter. "It feels good," another woman said, "I feel like [my
baby] is something I have the power to shape . . . and that
it's something that can't be taken away." Kathy Weingar-
ten, author of a similar study, concluded, "Their babies
were their own gifts to themselves." Carla Ramsey and
others like her chose motherhood as they chose their careers: after careful reflection and planning, but *for* themselves.

In so doing, single mothers by choice had revived an
ancient family structure that had been lost for nearly all of
recorded history: matriarchy. Since the late nineteenth-
century writings of J. J. Bachofen, anthropologists have
known of the existence of matriarchal societies in Meso-
potamia from roughly 9000 to 5000 B.C. From cave paint-
ings, potsherds and rare statuary, field workers have
determined that those cultures worshiped goddesses rather
than gods, and passed property from mother to child rather
than from father to son, in part, Bachofen and others specu-
late, because these ancient peoples did not understand the
male role in procreation. Childbearing seemed the mysteri-
ous power of women alone: a power worthy of worship
since it was this mystery which perpetuated society.

Destroyed by the emergence of "patriarchal" societies

which prayed to violent male gods rather than the benevolent fertility goddesses, the lost matriarchies are now mainly the fascination of a few cultural historians and feminist scholars. Some believe, along with the authors of *The Coming Matriarchy*, Elizabeth Nickles and Laura Ashcraft, that as women enter the corporate world, dethroning men from their seats of power in boardrooms and legislative chambers, the matriarchal order will once again be achieved. Yet if women like Carla Ramsey are the new Matriarchs, their power derives from an entirely different source than their prehistoric ancestors'. It was the increased availability of birth control in the 1960s that allowed women to join the work force in such large numbers in the 1970s. Only when their childbearing years could be regulated could women like Carla Ramsey expect to raise children *and* support them. It was not the mystery of childbirth, but a proven chemical formula, that returned women to a position of authority.

And the difference would prove to be crucial. I wanted to believe, as did so many single women, that with their careers and their children the new Matriarchs had all a woman needed from life. Yet listening to their stories, I only heard further evidence of the fears that ruled the Control Generation. As each one spoke, like Carla, with stoic pessimism about long-term love, I heard again the nagging fear of intimacy, the defensive accounting of the cost of loving, that so many single women shared. The only difference was that, like every parent, these women were banking on the future affection of their children. This would be the lasting love in their lives: but at what cost to both mother and child?

Birth control and the planned parenthood movement have been a boon to all women, allowing them to combine a career with the work of mothering. But should the end result have been this isolated, nearly asexual reproduction? As Carla Ramsey told me more about her life, I began to understand her choice of single motherhood not so much as a noble experiment in women's liberation, but as a courageous attempt to form a family of her own in the wake of the kind of tragedy that beset all too many families during the apparently peaceful 1950s.

A Mad Housewife

"When I was a child," Carla tells me, "I assumed, like every other girl I knew, that I was going to grow up and get married and have children and reproduce my mother's life. But by the time I was twenty, my mother's life had become a tragedy. She was an educated woman who didn't go to work after her children were born because my father didn't want her to. She lived in the suburbs and was tremendously frustrated, and after twenty-five years of that he divorced her. She had to go back into the work force and she was unprepared in every possible way, and it ended up literally killing her. She committed suicide less than a year after the divorce.

"I talked to her the day before she died. I had just been home for spring vacation, but I was back at USC, and I was going to my first formal dance in a fraternity house on campus. She'd bought me a dress while I was home, so she knew about the dance and I thought she'd called just to talk about that. I spent the whole conversation complaining about my dress and complaining about the party and complaining about everything. But I ended up having a good time at the dance and I was thinking about calling her the next morning to tell her how well it all turned out when I got the call saying that she was dead. I realized she must have called me the afternoon before to say good-bye.

"That was in 1965. She was a smart woman. She was the first of all her friends to read Betty Friedan and Simone de Beauvoir. But she didn't hang on long enough to find out that she was not the only woman in the world that this was happening to, that it was only natural to be suffering after my father had just fired her from the only job she had known for twenty-five years: housewife. She didn't stay alive long enough to see that she wasn't alone and that millions of other women would be confronting divorce in the next decade."

Carla's mother's lonely fate was not unusual. During the decades just after World War II, when so many families settled into America's quiet suburbs, the suicide rate for white women increased by an alarming 49 percent. Of the forty women in this study, two were the daughters of suicides. The mad housewife was no myth. And the conditions that produced her were everywhere.

Carla's family was a normal one for the 1950s, not so different from the Bensons of White Plains who raised the Loner, April. "On the most superficial level," Carla says, "everything in the household revolved around my father. He came from an old Yankee family, and even though we were living in a suburb south of San Francisco, he insisted on running the house in the old style. He was very autocratic. He was the kind of person who believed that respect only went up, it never came down. He was never wrong and never sorry. He loved us kids, but he didn't know very much about children, and he didn't have the remotest idea how to interact with a child successfully.

"That was left to my mother. She was a spectacular parent, whose main work became motherhood as her marriage shredded up on her. My mother always understood what I was going through, whatever it was. I always felt she hadn't forgotten at all what it was like to be a child. So in another sense, *my* family life and the lives of my two younger brothers revolved around my mother. My father was pretty much excommunicated—he didn't even speak our language. By the time I was conscious of what was going on between my parents it was clear that my mother was giving all her emotional energy to us, and withholding from him, for a whole history of reasons: mainly that he had a violent temper and she found it easier to fight back with silence. I think she also believed her role was to protect the children from his anger, because he could blow up over the slightest things. Something I was wearing, or something I was planning to do that he happened to hear about, could really set him off. By the time I was a teenager he was so buried in his work that those were the only things he noticed about me. He was so far out of my life, he didn't know what was normal for a teenaged girl to be doing. So my mother was something of a conspirator with me against my father. It wasn't a good idea, but it seemed like the only reasonable way to handle him."

The Ramseys' domestic politics were so commonplace they were the sort that millions were laughing over in sitcoms like *Leave It to Beaver* and *Father Knows Best*. Yet off the TV screen, the effects of such a divided family were disastrous. Carla tells me, "Certainly there is an absolute correlation between my feelings about marriage for myself and what I observed in that household. I feel that I never, never want to get into a situation of being too deeply involved with just one person. I don't feel it's safe. Because while my parents were very different, they were each other's only contact with the emotional world. They were asking too much of each other, and they solved it by giving nothing and getting even less. I don't think one person can carry that load. You need to spread it out a little, both the joy and the sorrow.

"Friends were the safety net that my mother lacked. She came from the generation where you didn't talk about things like your marriage and your feelings of depression with *anyone*. She was fifty when she was divorced, and fifty when she died. She was solidly in the middle of life. But she thought her life was finished—she was no longer attractive, her children were growing up. She believed she had nothing left. She thought she was doing us all a favor by killing herself because she was in such terrible shape that she was no use to anybody.

"Her suicide was an act of bravery and an act of illness. Her hope, of course, was that she would get to my father, and she didn't. She didn't get to him at all. At that level, it was utterly futile. But she did get to us, her children. And we were not the people she meant to get at all. What she did to us was a kind of betrayal that you never recover from."

The Survivor

After her mother's death, Carla sought refuge outside her shattered family. She returned to college, and stayed on for graduate school to get a master's degree in theater arts. "The university was a real racket," Carla says. "As a student I was only responsible to the five professors I saw each week, and the rest of the time I was getting a free ride in a closed community that offered just the right amount of psychological protection." Then for several years after graduation she worked as a publicist for a small theater company in West Los Angeles, an environment that seemed safely similar to college.

"I liked the physicality of theater work," Carla recalls. "People screamed, cried, laughed, put their arms around you, kissed you. I felt like I'd been with people all day, and if I came home alone at night and read a book or did the laundry, that was fine. I never felt lonely, because the theater gives you the sense that there's always a place to go. But after several years I began to realize that feeling was misleading. My work and my friendships were so intermingled that it took me a while to notice that my friendships never lasted longer than the run of the show. I wanted to do more with my life than work for a small-time theater—so I quit and started working here at the agency. That was twelve years ago. This place combined the liveliness of the theater with the stability of an office environment, and I've been happy in my job ever since."

Like all the single mothers I interviewed, Carla found security early on in her work and with friends, but never looked for it with a man. "In my early years in the theater and at the agency, I fell in love several times," Carla says, "usually with men I met through work. They were writers, actors, casting directors. But all the relationships ended, basically through drifting. One or the other of us, or both, would ultimately want to go our own way. I came to believe that relationships have a contained life-span, and 'forever' for one relationship might be a year or five years. But never 'forever' in that romantic, misty-eyed meaning of the word. I think my hopes for that forever kind of love were killed off in me when my mother died. I know I looked at things much more realistically afterward, without that gauzy cloud stuff."

Strangely, what was not killed off in Carla Ramsey's heart was her desire to become a mother. While Carla's mother so clearly suffered from the limitations of the housewife role, Carla did not, like so many of her generation, confuse the housewife role with motherhood. The closeness of mother and daughter that seemed oppressive to other women looked glorious to Carla once she had lost it. "I always knew I wanted to be a parent," Carla says. "I can't remember a time when I didn't want to be a mother, and the feeling only got stronger after my mother died. I wanted to be able to make somebody else feel about themselves the way my mother made me feel about myself. I wanted to reproduce that relationship because I had had it so successfully. I really wanted to be a mother of a daughter, and I lucked out with Kyra."

While working with a survivor's zeal to make her own life more stable, Carla had nevertheless accepted her mother's teachings on love: that children are a safer bet than men. A sensitive mother herself, Carla did not expect her daughter to take the place of a lover. But she had long ago lost faith in romantic love and failed to learn to assert her need for commitment from the men who seemed always to be drifting out of her life. Like the mediator Meredith, she feared the war between the sexes that she had seen so much more of than peace—and she preferred to keep her distance. She would be able to regulate the emotional climate of a single parent household more easily than any of the romances she had known. Like her mother, Carla Ramsey would reserve the nurturing "female part" of herself for her daughter.

"Because of my mother's example," Carla explains, "I never thought childbirth was going to be the culmination of some serious romantic passion. I really thought of parenthood as separate from the problems of keeping a love relationship going. In a lot of ways, it's easier not to have to worry about both at once. So it's always felt natural to me to be going about motherhood the way I have. And I am much more prepared to give twenty years of my life to my daughter than to a lover, because I know that if I do it right at all she will grow up and leave, but remain my friend. She will come back and visit me.

"I haven't dated anyone regularly since Kyra was born," Carla continues. "At first it was because I had more than I could handle, between working and taking care of her. And more recently, I haven't met anybody I'd care to spend a lot of time with. When it's a question of going out to dinner or to a movie, I'd rather be going with a good friend, or with Kyra. I have a full life. I'm never lonely, because basically I like being single. I think grown-ups have to live together in compromise in order to survive. I'm happy to compromise all day long at the office, but when I want to go to bed and eat pretzels, I don't want to ask anyone's permission.

"Besides Kyra, I don't really need anyone else. She made my house a home. She gave me a reason to come home, besides just catching up on my work. When I lived by myself, I spent most of my spare time reading scripts and making business calls. Now I'm part of a family. Since Kyra was born, I've never once questioned the meaning of my life. The meaning is to enrich my daughter's life, and to let her enrich mine. Kyra's birth and my mother's death are the two things that changed my life. I learned that the meaning of life is that you just live it—for the people you love, and who love you."

The Reproduction of Mothering

As I left Carla Ramsey's office, I was troubled by the thought that, of the forty women I interviewed, this woman who had lost her mother was one of the few who had become a mother herself. For those whose mothers continued to live out the old patterns of femininity, the maternal examples of discontent and self-sacrifice had been enough to turn a generation of women against their own gender.

In her 1978 book *The Reproduction of Mothering*, the psychologist Nancy Chodorow outlined her now widely accepted theory of the psychological development of women. Learning from their same sex parent, Chodorow wrote, little girls begin imitating mothering qualities in their earliest games and even with their friends. It is this mimicry that accounts for the difference between girls' and boys' play identified in Janet Lever's study. By the time a woman reaches adulthood, she is so well schooled in the arts of compassion and nurturing that these have become her chief traits, the "female part" of women that Meredith Gray described.

Yet in every woman's story so far I had heard the desperate yearning of the Control Generation not to relive but to reject their mother's way of life. Theirs was not the daughter's simple wish to be a better mother than her own had been. It was a radically new determination for women: the desire to repress the female qualities of caring that this generation believed its parents had foundered on.

It was in a different and more tragic sense that these women managed nonetheless to reproduce their mothers' lives: by seeking only a limited role in adulthood. Ellen Barnes, the Professional, chose work over love in a simple inversion of her mother's choice of love over work. Like her mother, April Benson, the Loner, dedicated herself to one occupation; her mother had chosen housewife, she chose sculptor. Carla Ramsey directly mimicked her mother by choosing mother love over romantic love. The women of the Control Generation easily pointed to the empty spaces in their mothers' lives, yet seemed unable to complete the jigsaw puzzle for themselves.

Through every self-protective choice made by this reform-minded generation ran the fear of the most basic and sustaining of human emotions: the love affair between men and women. The same women who broke off affairs complaining that men were unwilling to make commitments were, like Carla Ramsey, themselves disbelievers in "forever." Some, like April Benson and the Sexual Revolutionary Rikki Sanchez, learned distrust in early love affairs under the pressure of sexual freedom. For others, like

Carla, Meredith Gray and Beth Phillips, doubt had stayed with them since witnessing in childhood the surrender of their own mothers to the men in their lives. The women of the Control Generation worried on every date that a man might claim some part of themselves that would later cost them their independence. And so they left the domain of the heart uncharted.

Of the forty women, the Caretakers had achieved the easiest balance in their lives. Until her recent breakup, Beth Phillips maintained a placid homelife with her live-in boyfriend. Meredith Gray thrived on the knowledge that her clients depended on her advice and concern each week. And Carla Ramsey lived to be needed by her daughter. These three women had learned to channel the female part of themselves in safe directions. Yet Beth's tame romance and Meredith's vicariously experienced emotional life told me how far they were from releasing their deepest feelings of love and compassion. Carla had turned a bitter legacy into a life-sustaining love for her child. But like her mother, she had no hopes for lasting love in her own life.

As members of the Control Generation we failed to recognize that we would remain childlike as long as we lived in the shadow of our mother's failings. We believed in the wisdom of putting off marriage and motherhood, the commitments that had sidetracked an earlier generation, and devoted ourselves to self-fulfillment. Yet unknowingly we denied ourselves fulfillment by postponing the lessons that would have come with risking ourselves in love. For many women, delaying marriage made it no easier: in our thirties, independent and self-supporting, we felt we had even more to lose. Until we thought of how much we had denied ourselves out of fear.

PART V
Marriage: The New Risk

"I'd better tell you right away," Franny Larsen announced apologetically as she let me into her Manhattan condominium, "I'm not going to be single for long. I'm getting married in the spring." The news caught me off guard since, when I'd arranged the interview less than a month before, Franny, an account executive with an advertising agency in midtown, had said nothing about marriage. She mentioned only that she had a boyfriend in Milwaukee, and that the commute was getting to be more than her emotions or her pocketbook could withstand.

But then, Franny was not alone in her interest in marriage. More than half of the single women I'd spoken with had told me they would like to marry. Even though they were uncertain about how to look for involvement and often felt terrified of finding it, women everywhere seemed ready to move beyond the limited challenge of proving their independence. Yet I was to learn from Franny that the fears of compromise and self-sacrifice that I'd heard expressed so often would not end with an engagement. In fact, her wedding plans had sent Franny Larsen into a far deeper round of worries.

Nordic-looking with her straw-blond hair and deep blue eyes, Franny seemed distinctly uncomfortable as we sat together on the gray wool couch in her tastefully furnished living room. As we talked, her eyes constantly scanned the room as if to make an inventory of all her possessions: the antique lamps, Persian throw rugs and lithographs she had chosen with obvious care. She did this not, as so many women had, as the proud owner, but more as the sorry leavetaker, checking once more through all she would have to give up. For Franny had decided to leave her secure job and beloved apartment in New York for an uncertain employment future and her fiancé's unfamiliar household in Milwaukee. Franny told me that all her important life decisions had involved long-distance moves. The prospect of this one called up memories of a long flight to the freedom that now she was frightened of losing.

Growing up on a prosperous dairy farm in southern Minnesota, Franny Larsen was the only daughter of a much-respected small businessman. But as a girl, Franny felt the open spaces on the farm only mocked the tight limits on her life. "My family always represented intellectual bondage to me," Franny recalls. "They never cared what I thought. They tried to raise me to be a sweet, passive, soft-spoken country girl—and I wasn't."

The Larsens' gentle efforts to pacify their only child turned decidedly harsher during her freshman year at Bryn Mawr College in Pennsylvania. "When I left home for the first time," Franny told me, "I thought I had won my freedom. But that was the year of Kent State, when students even at a quiet women's college were holding antiwar teach-ins and demonstrations. Politically I'm every bit as conservative as my parents, and they knew that. But I've always been a person with a lot of curiosity. If something's going on around me, I want to understand it. So I called home and told them I wanted to stay on at school for a few days after the end of the spring semester and listen to the speeches at the demonstrations. There was dead silence on the phone. Two days later, my mother arrived on campus, and while I took my final exams, she packed my bags.

When we got home my parents informed me that I was not going back to Bryn Mawr. That was a long, hot summer."

Later, Franny would learn to be more cautious about bucking her parents' authority, but not before another unpleasant lesson. "My parents sent me to the University of Wisconsin," Franny continued, "which wasn't any safer as far as the student movement was concerned. But to them it was a whole lot closer to home and that was what counted. I joined a sorority, and I made good grades, and did everything just right, so that when I had the chance to join a touring student theater company in my senior year, I thought I had every right to go my own way. Joining that group was the hardest thing I ever did. My parents were dead set against it. They thought I'd be exposed to drugs and sex and all kinds of evil things that of course I'd been living with for years on campus. I had to stand up for myself and just get beaten by my family, emotionally. I found out later they had me followed the whole time by a private detective!

"I stuck it out for a whole year, but in the end I just couldn't take any more of their silences and their disapproval. I told them I would give up theater if I could move to New York and find myself a real job. They were stunned. Their idea of my life was still that I would be married within a month of graduation. They weren't going to relax until some nice man was taking care of their helpless daughter. But they went along with the plan because it meant I'd quit touring with the group. At least I'd be in one place, and they visited New York City often enough so that they could keep an eye on me. I didn't care if they were checking up. At least I would have a chance to live a life of my own."

Like many women from sheltered backgrounds, Franny would find that the chance to be self-reliant was only the beginning of a struggle for independence. "My father found me my first job, a nice safe one in an ad agency where an old college friend of his was a partner," Franny recalled. "But even so it's a miracle I wasn't fired. I behaved like a spoiled brat. It was like having a little girl in the office—

that's what my parents had raised me to be. I had no sense of how to behave in the business world. I was a classic case of a young, unprepared woman demanding to be accepted as a professional with no idea of how to prove herself. And I made every mistake in the book. I expected everyone to listen to my brilliant ideas from the start, and I would throw tantrums if they didn't. That didn't get me too far."

It took Franny many years and several job changes to find her place in the advertising world. But ultimately the spoiled little girl turned into a professional known for her witty ad copy and her ability to attract clients. Now Franny says, however, that she is grateful for those years on her own, not just for the training in her profession, but for the chance to grow up in ways her parents' program for Franny Larsen would never have permitted.

"I learned a lot in the business world," Franny explained, "but what self-sufficiency really gave me was years of freedom to have a lot of relationships with different men. That is where I've done a lot of growing, fighting through troubled affairs and learning by my mistakes. I realize now that I would subconsciously pick each man for a particular need. Then I'd outgrow the need. With my first boyfriend, we fought a great deal, and I learned a lot about what I would never do again. I would never berate anybody, I would never be a bitch again. The next man was mild-mannered and would never ever fight. But he wasn't terribly bright. My *next* boyfriend was a genius, a surgeon, but he was off in the clouds. Then finally I met Tony, my fiancé. He represents what I know I need now—and for a long time to come. He's very self-reliant, and so am I by now. I'm ready to stand on my own two feet and still be married. And he'll give me the latitude to do that."

In deciding to marry, Franny had to confront what the women of the Control Generation viewed as a woman's fundamental conflict: whether to give up her independence for a man. It was a conflict that had been part of Franny's life for many years before she felt ready to "stand on my own two feet and still be married." And it would not easily be put to rest. As it had for so many women, the conflict presented itself to Franny as a choice about whether to follow the man she loved.

Tony Barnet was not the first of Franny's out-of-town lovers. "Since I was twenty-five, I have not dated anyone who lived in this city," Franny said. "I've been on the road practically every weekend for five years." At first the long distances suited her; she could have intimacy in small doses without jeopardizing her hard-won freedom. "I was leading my own life," Franny continued. "That meant so much to me I wouldn't compromise it for anything. I backed off from marriage every time. I see the same thing in a lot of my professional friends. We've gone through so many fights inside ourselves or directly with parents or lovers over what we should be allowed to do that it makes us fierce in our desire to be independent—and angry when anyone asks us to compromise. I was told how to grow up instead of being allowed to grow up—and as a result my freedom means a great deal to me."

But by age thirty, when Franny met Tony, a young Milwaukee businessman who'd come to New York to visit mutual friends from Franny's University of Wisconsin days, she began to feel differently. "Before, I wasn't grown up enough to accept a long-term relationship," Franny told me. "But suddenly I was secure enough in my job not to feel threatened. I knew I had proven skills, and that I was viewed by my colleagues as a professional. And Tony would never ask me to stop working—he respects my professional abilities. So I was free in a new way. For the first time I wanted to spend *more* time with someone the closer we got, rather than less. It dawned on me that while I've always had one boyfriend at a time, my relationships last only about two years. When they get right down to the most crucial point of making a commitment, I draw back. This time I've decided not to let that happen."

The commuting relationship, which once suited Franny perfectly, began for the first time to feel strained and disappointing. Even before the two discussed marriage, Franny began to think about leaving New York. "Tony had started a business in Milwaukee and there was no way he could move," Franny explained. "Whereas I had skills that were transferable. It's definitely scary to think of hitting the pavement in a whole new town, but that wasn't what held me back. What really bothered me was that I was afraid of the way it would look. I was sure my friends and colleagues would see me as just another woman who gave up her job to follow a man. I couldn't shake it—I suppose because I half believed it too. But then I started asking myself, why should I give up the person I care most about in the world just to keep up an image?"

Tony and Franny had been commuting for nearly a year when, one night in Wisconsin, Franny admitted she'd been thinking of staying on. Tony, always more eager for marriage than Franny, took the opportunity to propose, and Franny agreed immediately. But back in Manhattan, with Tony nearly a thousand miles away and the wedding four months off, the fears started again. Much as Franny reminded herself that Tony couldn't leave Milwaukee, that she would still have her work and her freedom, nothing could change the fact that she was making a choice that women have learned to scorn in the past decade.

"Options are pressure," Franny told me grimly. "Ten years ago I would have said that I'm thankful to be living in a time when women have so many choices. But choices give women a lot of responsibility we aren't used to. That's why it's easiest for most of us to stick with one thing—one job, one city. When we try something new, we really don't have anyone to blame but ourselves if it doesn't work out. I know how I behave when I'm by myself—but I don't know how I'll start behaving when there's someone else around. I know what I've got here in New York—a great job, a wonderful apartment, and a lover on weekends and vacations. But I don't even know whether the relationship I'm giving it all up for will survive once we're together seven days a week.

"I'm scared to death. This is the major turning point in my life. I go through periods of depression and stark fear—and moments of elation. I feel terribly threatened about the loss of my personal freedom. I tell myself this is just an experiment—I'm going to see how I do. I'm going through with it. I'm going to get married, after years of fearing it."

The Cost of Loving

Franny Larsen was not alone in her decade-long flight from marriage. In 1970, the year after her parents brought her home from Bryn Mawr, the U.S. Census showed a one-third increase of unmarried women under the age of twenty-four. Women were postponing marriage at such a rate that within the next six years the average marriage age rose higher than in any decade since 1890. As the number of Americans under age thirty-five living alone skyrocketed, increasing more than 200 percent between 1970 and 1980, population analysts could only confirm what millions of young women already knew: marriage was no longer woman's favored route to adulthood.

Like Franny, women had come to value an independence they believed could be achieved only outside marriage. If they planned to marry at all, it would be after years spent proving themselves in the working world, getting to know themselves in ways they presumed marriage would prevent. Once a source of security and the confirmation of womanhood, marriage had come to seem almost life-threatening. Some women developed persistent marriage phobias, like the thirty-one-year-old writer who told me, "I always cry at weddings. People think I'm being emotional—happy for the couple, or even envious. But I'm not. With every word the minister says—'faith,' 'honor,' 'commitment'—it's like he's pounding nails into a coffin."

How did independence come to mean staying single? As with every important liberation movement, the impulse for the women's movement had to come from a critique of unjust institutions; the first to come under fire was marriage. Looking for an explanation for woman's failure to assert herself in the public arenas of politics and the professions when she had been emancipated for decades, writers from Friedan to Millett singled out the economic dependence that marrriage fostered in women during the 1950s and 1960s and that so often led to psychological dependence as well.

Although not all feminists recommended breaking the wedding vows, many of the most vocal leaders did. Perhaps the most devastating critique came in *The Second Sex*, first published in the United States in 1952. Here Simone de Beauvoir described marriage as a chiefly economic arrangement, with husband providing his wife financial support in exchange for her household labor. This might have been an equitable arrangement, de Beauvoir argued, except that the couple lived in a society in which working for a paycheck gives a man freedom and respect while "woman's work within the home gives her no autonomy; it is not directly useful to society, it does not open out on the future, it produces nothing. . . . The situation must be changed by prohibiting marriage as a 'career' for woman."

Continuing the economic critique of marriage in her 1970 *The Female Eunuch*, Germaine Greer wrote, "If women are to effect a significant amelioration in their condition it seems obvious that they must refuse to marry. No worker can be required to sign on for life: if [she] did, [her] employer could disregard all [her] attempts to gain better pay and conditions." It didn't take long for the association of marriage and economic slavery to become shorthand: "I have a very clear, keen memory of myself the day after I was married," Adrienne Rich wrote in the 1976 *Of Woman Born*. "I was sweeping a floor."

It was left to the psychiatrists, however, to make the crucial connection between marriage and the loss of self that the Control Generation so feared. In a frequently reprinted 1971 article titled "Phobias After Marriage," the psychiatrist Alexandra Symonds summoned up the nightmares of the generation when she described housewives "who seem to shrivel up after getting married, who seem to lose all interests and involvements, who constrict their inner life, and who become depressed, anxious, and excessively dependent [because] they feared the consequences of taking life into their own hands." The words of feminist writers and psychologists combined to present a challenge to the new generation: young women must take their lives back.

As the women of the Control Generation went off to work, determined to know the power of the pocketbook and so to know themselves, they learned to fear more than marriage. They came to distrust the nice men, the in-town lovers, the marrying kind who might make them into wives. They learned to fear intimacy as the first step toward an involvement out of which they might never manage to extricate themselves. And they learned to fear the "female part" of themselves that might be moved to care for a man deeply enough to halt them in their flight to freedom.

For even as they promoted the cause of women in the workplace, the early feminist critics of marriage accepted society's devaluation of woman's special capacity for caretaking. In adopting the paycheck as a measure of self-worth, Greer, de Beauvoir and others implicitly labeled the female talent for nurturance a weakness at best and evidence of collusion with the male enemy at worst. Women who followed their advice pursued only the traits that succeed in the marketplace—diligence, rationality and agression—and that, women soon proved, could belong to either sex. Without these traits women were lost in a society that valued wage-earning; yet by limiting their aspirations to worldly success, the women of the Control Generation were seeking a self that was genderless. And women would find they had paid an unexpected price for this new selfhood, this unprecedented freedom. In counting the cost of loving, they had deprived themselves of full lives as adults.

In their thirties, the women of the Control Generation had reached a crisis they had expected to pass through years before. An identity crisis was afflicting the Brave New Women, the Self-Seekers and Caretakers who once believed they had all the answers. For female identity, they had at last discovered, could not be revealed by willing it in isolation, by evading connections, by repeatedly pulling back from intimacy to reassure themselves of their autonomy. The very connections they had avoided might have been their best pathways to self-discovery.

Confronting this new crisis, some began, in a startling about-face, to envy their mothers: women who had stayed home to raise families and then joined the work force in middle age. Finding work late in life may have been difficult, but now they had both jobs and families, their workaholic daughters mourned. Other women admitted they had begun to doubt the wisdom of waiting so long to marry. Some even idealized their parents' impetuous courtships and early weddings. "My parents met at a dance and—bang!—they knew they were meant for each other," said one woman, a veteran of ten years in bank management and as many love affairs. "Maybe they had their differences over the years, but they worked them out. The marriage was always more important than either one of them individually, and there wasn't any agonizing over priorities."

Part of this new envy is nostalgia for a time these women never knew, when a woman's choices were clear and limited, and when, as Franny Larsen says, women took less responsibility for their lives. But that nostalgia arises from a voice deep inside us that should not be ignored: the female voice that asks to love and be loved, the voice of a caring self that finds no adequate outlet in the world of business. It is this voice that we silenced in our headlong rush for success, and in our eagerness to reinvent womanhood.

Because of the idealistic battles the Control Generation fought and won, we live in a time when women have more choices and can accomplish far more than ever before in America. Yet we have also created an era in which men and women both have grown uncertain of their gender identity, when the best-selling books of the day tell us what "real men" and "real women" do and don't do because we, ourselves, don't know the answers. Men and women both have given their hearts not to lovers and children but to careers that in the end must dehumanize us if they are all we have. For women to learn to reconcile their anger at past injustices and their need to prove themselves with the rhythms of human life and love—this is our new challenge.

The Future of the Control Generation

I dialed the Milwaukee number Franny Larsen had given me at the close of our interview. Now it was almost a year after our first meeting, six months after the date of her wedding to Tony Barnet. Remembering her fear of trading away her independence I half expected to hear a male voice tell me Franny had given up her wedding plans and stayed in New York. Worse still was the possibility that Franny herself would answer, telling me her impulsive decision to leave New York for the unknowns of marriage and Milwaukee had somehow backfired. After all, she had known Tony for only a year, and during that time she'd only seen him on weekends.

But the woman who answered the phone as Franny Barnet sounded decidedly more cheerful than the Franny Larsen I had spoken with the year before. Her relaxed tone told me more than her simple words describing the life she had been leading since her wedding the past spring. Franny said she had taken her time settling into Milwaukee. She was free-lancing as a PR consultant, and working on the house and in the garden in spare moments. And, she admitted with some surprise, "the issue of independence hasn't crossed my mind much. In fact I feel damned independent having broken away from the nine-to-five rat race in New York. I love working my own hours, and I feel much more in command of my life than I ever did getting a weekly paycheck.

"I had been working practically every day of my life since I was twenty-one," Franny continued. "That's ten years. And to tell the truth, I've found out a lot more about myself than I ever would have if I'd stayed in New York. I've had the time to find out the things I really like to do, and simply to appreciate my homelife. I like working at home, and spending most of my spare time around the house with Tony. What has changed the most, though, are my feelings for Tony. We are closer, *profoundly* closer than I ever imagined two people could be."

Both Franny and I puzzled over the fears she had voiced so strongly a year ago. Would there have been any way to avoid them? Franny offered, "I wish there was some way to tell women that they will be exactly the same human beings after they get married as before. I think it might help a lot of women decide whether or not they want to marry. In my case, we were two people who got along before, and we're getting along still—only more so. In most ways I feel the same as I did when I was single. But I'm actually working better and thinking more clearly. Marriage hasn't intruded on my work at all. I feel a lot more settled and I don't feel I've given anything up for that. In fact, I've never felt freer."

The women of the Control Generation held fast to higher ambitions than any generation of women in recent history: they hoped to become lawyers, doctors, artists, musicians. They planned to change the mores of their society; they even hoped to save the world. And some of this they accomplished. Yet for so many women, these high ideals were based on early disappointments. They had seen, in their mothers' lives, the destructive power of love when it becomes a woman's single reason for living. They had been raised by women who extended the caretaking role to the point where they had sacrificed themselves and alienated their daughters. The women of the Control Generation spent years trying to convince themselves that one-night stands and out-of-town lovers were all they needed before they discovered, as Franny Larsen did, that love could support women rather than overwhelm them.

And even then, the Myth of Independence had played so powerfully on women's fears that many would carry their doubts into marriage, never learning the interdependence that a healthy marriage requires. The divorce rate would always be high for those who continued, like the Professional Ellen Barnes, to give less of themselves at home than at the office, or who believed, along with the Heroine Laurie MacVey, that selfhood could be found only outside marriage.

But there were women, too, like Franny, who were ready to learn, who would come to marriage from independence, impatient with singleness and secure enough in their self-knowledge to risk joining their lives with another's. For these women the bonds of commitment could actually be liberating. One thirty-four-year-old woman, a painter, told me she had suffered from insomnia for the five years before her recent marriage. Even during the three years she shared an apartment with the man she would ultimately marry, she said, "I could never be certain of a full night's sleep. Something deep inside me was unsettled. Since the wedding all that has changed. I sleep like a log, and whatever it was inside me that was troubled has never bothered me again."

Another woman, a thirty-year-old social worker, told me, "From the time I was a teenager, I never believed I would find love. There were so many divorces in my parents' circle that my friends and I stopped believing in romance along with Santa Claus. In my twenties I had several long relationships, but I was always fighting men off, expecting to be disappointed. Finally last year I took a risk, and decided to marry the man I'd been seeing for several years. We had always been good together. But there was the underlying tension—where is the relationship going? What does each of us want? Now that we're married, there's no question about any of that. And instead there is all this love that I never thought I'd have. It's as if I'd been blessed."

Marriage will never be the panacea that our mothers were taught it would be in the 1950s. Marriages will continue to end in divorce for all the old reasons, and for the new ones stemming from our current devotion to the single life. Yet we must now prove that our new selfhood runs deeper than simple competence in the material world. We must permit ourselves to believe in the long-term love that a good marriage protects, and to discover that love teaches us as much about ourselves as does solitude. For the human self does not exist in isolation. We must find others to care for, and who will care for us, making ourselves full members of a community with far greater boundaries than the professional world. Only then will we have discovered ourselves as women.